All the Blessings and Benedictions in the Bible

A study of all the biblical references to blessings and benedictions

To: Mike Harland
God's Blessing to Many
Jim Harvey
12/18/18

Jim Harvey

All the Blessings and Benedictions in the Bible

A study of all the biblical references to blessings and benedictions

Copyright © 2018 by Jim Harvey

....

....

Scriptures: *Holman Christian Standard Bible*
                 The New King James Version

....

Library of Congress Control Number: 2018941121
ISBN-13:   Paperback: 978-1-64151-700-3

....

Printed in the United States of America

LitFire
PUBLISHING

LitFire LLC
1-800-511-9787
www.litfirepublishing.com
order@litfirepublishing.com

Contents

DEDICATION V

FOREWORD VII

PREFACE IX

INTRODUCTION 1

All the BLESSINGS
and BENEDICTIONS in the Bible 1

I. Old Testament References to Blessings and Benedictions 5

II. New Testament References to Blessings and Benedictions.............78

Conclusion.. 112

Songs for the study of
"Bible Blessings and Benedictions" 115

"Bless His Holy Name" 116

"There Shall Be Showers of Blessing" 117

"Blessed Be The Name" 118

"Count Your Blessings" 119

DEDICATION

Dedicated to all those many family and friends who have been God's means of blessing me through these years of such a blessed life.

OTHER BOOKS BY JIM AND VAL HARVEY

Seize the Day with Yahweh

What a Difference a Name Makes

Who Changed God's Name?

God's Little Things

Lord, Teach Us to Pray

Helping Christians Discover Their Gifts for Ministry

Study Helps for a five volume study series
by Charles Swindoll:

Growing Deeper in the Christian Life

FOREWORD

by Robert P. Lambert,

Professor of Marketing
Belmont University, Nashville, Tennessee

We are blessed by God in so many ways. All good things come from God and so when we receive blessings, why shouldn't we thank Him for them? In the Bible we can find the words *bless, blessing* and *blessed* more than 580 times. Similarly, a benediction is a declaration of blessings from God upon His loved ones. Benedictions also are found throughout the Bible. Benedictions, though brief, offer words of assurance or precepts designed to bring joy, peace, comfort, and security to those who place their trust in God. Benedictions can be a remarkable source of healing because the words themselves are life.

The words *bless,* **blessed** and *blessing* are wonderful words. Christians use these words frequently, and most of the time we mean it. **Blessed** is a Christian word. It is a spiritual word. It is a biblical word. And it has been hijacked by our culture. People may talk about blessings in their lives, but the nonbeliever has no idea what a real blessing is, because only the child of God truly knows what it is to be blessed. It is also worth noting that Jesus both began and concluded His earthly ministry blessing people.

I did not always understand the meaning and nature of blessings because I was born into poverty on a sugar cane plantation in Louisiana along with 10 siblings. My parents were not educated, my father was a farm laborer, and our housing was substandard—no running water, electricity, heat, etc. Furthermore, birthdays and many holidays were not celebrated as most people did simply because we had no means to do so. So for the first 13 years of my life, blessings seemed to not apply to our family. Then, one of the most tragic events imaginable occurred—my mother died of a massive heart attack at age 49, and from that point on, God blessed me in ways that I could never have imagined.

Dr. Harvey has painstakingly and meticulously spent years researching *blessings and benedictions* in the Bible. He has artfully and masterfully written this book in a way that that is simple yet thought provoking. Dr. Harvey presents key Bible verses in his book of blessings and benedictions and gives detailed explanations and examples of their meaning. Reading this book has not only opened my eyes to a topic about which I had never given serious thought, it has also helped me understand that even when I was a child and it seemed like our family was cursed rather than blessed, God was there blessing us. This book has also caused me to be more deliberate in recognizing that all that I have comes from God and that every day is a blessing and gift. One of my favorite benedictions highlighted in Dr. Harvey's book comes from Ephesians 3:20-21 "Now to Him who is able to do exceedingly abundantly above all that we ask or think, according to the power that works in us, to Him be glory in the church by Christ Jesus throughout all ages, world without end. Amen." I have been blessed to be part of Dr. Harvey's Bible Study on Blessings and Benedictions. He truly lives what he writes and teaches, and brings to life the phrase "it is a blessing to give rather than receive." This book is a must read—it will be a blessing to you.

PREFACE

My interest in benedictions began as a young member of the First Christian Church in my home town of Hobart, Oklahoma. At the close of each worship service the pastor would dismiss us with a spoken benediction, either from the Bible or his own composition. I remember the effect these words had upon me as I felt sent out with God's promise of His favor upon me as I sought to fulfill His mission.

Many years later, as a pastor, I resumed this practice and noticed how the congregation responded with appreciation for this closing commission. More recently I have looked for some book that included all the Bible benedictions, with comments regarding their context and meaning. Since I could not find such a volume, I decided to compose this one.

As for the subject of Bible blessings, my career as a college professor of biblical studies led me to pursue various topics of interest in the Scriptures. And one of these subjects was that of the numerous and varied references to the role of blessings, especially God's blessings upon His people at various times. I was impressed with these expressions of God's favor upon selected leaders, enabling them to fulfill His assigned missions.

I have discovered that a blessing from God was far more than words of affirmation; when He blessed a person, they had a fresh anointing of power and ability. He was equipping them to perform some specific task.

In other words a blessing, from the biblical perspective had substance to it—the power to perform.

These studies also helped me better understand the significant relationship between blessings and benedictions in this sense: a spoken benediction is often a statement of God's favor, which is a declaration of His blessing. Again, benedictions and blessings go together—they are each a part of the whole.

My prayer is that God's Holy Spirit will open your understanding to have a greater appreciation for this subject. And that you will join me is expressing both blessings and benedictions to others.

INTRODUCTION

All the BLESSINGS
and BENEDICTIONS in the Bible

A study of all the biblical references to blessings and benedictions

Purpose for this study: to assist learners in gaining an awareness of the various occurrences of the many spoken and written blessings and benedictions found in the Scriptures in order to claim them for personal benefits and to share them with others.

Let's begin with several basic definitions:

Yahweh (pronounced YAH-way) This Hebrew word, in English letters, is God's preferred name which was first given to Moses at the burning bush. When God appeared to Moses, sending him back to Egypt to lead His people out of their bondage, Moses said, "If I go to the Israelites and say to them: the God of your fathers has sent me to you, and they ask me, 'What is His name?' what should I tell them?" God replied to Moses, "**I AM WHO I AM**. This is what you are to say to the Israelites: I AM has sent me to you." God also said to Moses, "Say to the Israelites **Yahweh**,

1

the God of you fathers, the God of Abraham, the God of Isaac, and the God of Jacob, has sent me to you. This is my name forever: **this is how I am to be remembered in every generation**.'" (Exodus 3:1-15)

Adding to the gravity of this name is the fact that the term Yahweh is the most frequently occurring noun in the entire Old Testament— some 6,828 times! But even more noteworthy than the name itself is its meaning, which is "to be." God was revealing to His servant Moses that He was the God who always has been, who is, and who always will be— the eternal I AM. And by revealing this unique name, God was assuring Moses that whatever he needed to be and do what God required, He was always with Moses as the One who would be all Moses needed—I AM.

Yahweh has many titles, such as Father, Lord, Master, Creator, Redeemer, Savior, Almighty God, and more. But He has just one name: Yahweh (I AM). Many translations of the Bible use the term LORD to translate Yahweh, but His true name is Yahweh.

In addition to this very significant truth is the fact that *Jesus* is the English translation of the Greek name for God's Son. However, His Hebrew name is *Yeshua,* which means "Yahweh is salvation," or "I AM salvation." When the angel told Joseph that Mary would have a son, he said, "You shall call His name Jesus, for He will save His people from their sins" (Matt. 1:21).

You may remember that on numerous occasions Jesus revealed truths about Himself using the term "I AM," such as "I AM the Bread of Life," "I AM the Light of the World," "I AM the Good Shepherd," "I AM the way, the truth and the Life," "I AM the resurrection and the life"—a total of nine times in John's writings. In each of these Jesus identified Himself with His Father, Yahweh (I AM). And He was saying to us, "I AM whatever you need to be and do all that pleases Me."

Benediction This word is not found in the Bible. However it best describes the occurrences of those expressions of God's favor upon His people. *Benediction* is a combination of two Latin words meaning "to speak good." So, a benediction is a statement of God's blessing (favor) upon His people. In other words, a benediction is a spoken expression of divine grace. There are more than 60 recorded benedictions in the Bible. (Some of these are expressions of blessing from God's servants upon others, such as Paul's many benedictions in his writings.)

Blessing As stated above, a blessing is a declaration of favor, either from God, or from one person to another. The Hebrew term most often translated "bless" or "blessing" is *barak*, meaning to fill with benefits. Some form of this word occurs over 500 times in the Old Testament. The New Testament Greek term is *makarios,* meaning "blessed," " fortunate," or "happy," and is found 50 times. Such a large number of uses indicates the significance of this concept of God's favor being shown in the context of a personal relationship with Him.

Most biblical occurrences of this term indicate a meaning that goes beyond mere words. A blessing is the bestowal of favor that enables the recipient to be a blessing to others, in other words, there is substance to the blessing—an ability to bless others. Consider this acrostic:

> **B**-Bestowing
>
> **L**-Love to
>
> **E**-Equip us for
>
> **S**- Selfless
>
> **S**- Service to others

Instructions for use of the Study Guides

Each section of study is followed by a suggested guide for encouraging both individuals and groups of students to respond to assignments and questions related to the materials covered in that section. These are designed to encourage further thought and discussion. You will note that the intended outcome of these studies is to grow in one's awareness of

God's current blessings as well as to motivate learners to bless others by reaching out to them in practical ways of service.

Suggestions for using the various songs located at the back of this book.

Both individual and groups of learners will profit by singing the selected hymns that have been added to this study. These and many other songs give expression to the fact of God's favor to us.

Now, we move to the numerous references to these special terms as found in the Scriptures. Both the New King James Translation and the Holman Christian Standard Bible Translation are used in this study.

I. Old Testament References to Blessings and Benedictions

GENESIS

We begin our Bible study with selected references to "bless," "blessing," or "blessed" in the Book of Genesis. There are over 80 of these; more than in any other book of the Bible except the Psalms. I find this rather significant that the first book of the Scriptures abounds with references to God reaching out to pronounce favor upon His creation. The remainder of His Word reveals the amazing way in which He expresses this grace.

1:22 Here is the first biblical occurrence of the term "bless." On the fifth day of creation, after forming all the creatures of the sea and birds of the air—the first living forms, "God **blessed** them, 'Be fruitful, multiply, and fill the waters of the seas, and let birds multiply on the earth.'" This initial blessing was to enable His living creatures to reproduce.

1:27-28 The second blessing is similar to the first in that the text states, "So God created man in His own image; He crated him in the image of God; He created them male and female. God **blessed** them, and God said to them 'Be fruitful, multiply, fill the earth and subdue it.'" In addition to reproducing, humankind was given authority over all living creatures. This dominion was part of God's blessing to them. (In Gen. 5:2 this **blessing** upon Adam and Eve is restated.)

Notice in both of these first references, God was enabling His creatures to do something very significant—to reproduce, to multiply, to pass on to others what they had received—life and the capacity to give life to others. They were blessed so they could be a blessing!

An old song expresses this truth as follows:

Have you had a kindness shown? Pass it on.

'Twas not meant for you alone. Pass it on.

Let it travel down the years; till in heaven the deed appears. Pass it on.

2:1-3 ". . . God **blessed** the seventh day and declared it holy, for on it He rested from His work of creation." Here is the first blessing from God on something that was not living—the seventh day. Later this became the fourth of the Ten Commandments: "Remember the seventh day and keep it holy." To say God blessed the seventh day certainly means that this day is to have special meaning to His people—a day set apart -- given to rest and renewal in order to perform the works He gives on the other six days. We would do well to take this principle more seriously, whether observing rest on Saturday or some other day, once each week. Christians have traditionally set apart (sanctified) the first day of the week (1 Cor. 16:1-2) to celebrate God's rest from His finished work of redemption through the resurrection of Jesus on the first day of the week.

Most of the remaining references to "blessings" in Genesis focus on God's blessing of individuals, as follows:

9:2 "So God **blessed** Noah and his sons and said to them, 'Be fruitful and multiply and fill the earth.'" This occurred after the flood had destroyed all living creatures except those on the ark with Noah and his family. God restated His original plan to populate the earth with offspring from one man and his wife. They had been spared to be a blessing.

12:2-3 Abraham was chosen by God to be the first Hebrew, the patriarch of all Jews. In this very significant passage, God blessed Abraham by establishing His covenant with Him and His descendants. "I will make you into a great nation, I will **bless** you. I will make your name great; and you shall be a **blessing**. I will **bless** those who **bless** you, and I will curse him who curses you, all the peoples of the earth shall be **blessed** through you." Here is a clear reference to a special descendant of Abraham, namely Jesus, by whom all the families of the earth would be blessed.

14:18-20 Melchizedek is described at the king of Salem and the priest of God Most High. In this passage we are told that he blessed Abram and said: "Abram is **blessed** by God Most High, Creator of heaven and earth; and I will give praise to God Most High who has handed over your enemies to your." Thus Melchizedek gave a two-fold blessing—one to Abram and a second to God. Here is the first mention of a person blessing God, an action that is repeated often in Scripture.

17:16,20 This chapter is filled with God's covenant promises to Abram, as well as God changing his name to Abraham, and the changing of his wife Sarai's name to Sarah. He went on to say, "I will **bless** her, indeed, I will give you a son by her. I will **bless** her and she will produce nations; kings of peoples will come from her." Again, God promised to bless Sarah that she might become the fountainhead of blessing to future generations. She was blessed to be a blessing.

22:16-18 God tested Abraham by ordering him to offer his son Isaac as a sacrifice. When Abraham indicated he would obey God, Isaac was spared and a lamb became his substitute. Then Yahweh said to him, "Because you have done this thing, and have not withheld your son, your only son, I will indeed **bless** you and make your offspring as numerous as the stars of the sky and the sands of the seashore . . . and all the nations of the earth shall be **blessed** by your offspring because you have obeyed my command." Here is a clear promise of the coming Messiah—Jesus, who would indeed bless all nations of the earth.

24:60 Abraham sent his servant back to his original home to seek a wife for his son Isaac. The term blessed occurs several times during this episode. One particular expression is of special interest. When Rebekah's family agreed for her to go back with Abraham's servant and become Isaac's wife, they blessed her with the first occurrence of a **benediction** in Genesis: "They blessed Rebekah, saying to her: 'Our sister, may you become thousands upon ten thousands. May your offspring possess the gates of their enemies.'" Here is a clear example of a spoken blessing. This **benediction** was ultimately fulfilled through her direct descendant, our Lord Jesus.

25:11; 26:3-4 "After Abraham's death, God **blessed** his son Isaac . . . 'I will be with you and **bless** you. For I will give all these lands to you and your offspring, and I will confirm the oath that I swore to your father Abraham. And I will make your offspring as numerous as the stars of the sky; I will give to your offspring all these lands, and all the nations of the earth will be **blessed** by your offspring.'" God's covenant with Abraham was thus passed on to his son Isaac. "Your seed" includes Jesus and all we who have trusted Him.

27:1-46 **There are some 21 occurrences in this chapter to the term "bless" or "blessing**." All referring to Isaac's bestowal of his patriarchal blessing on his first-born son. Thus this blessing belonged to Esau, however, his younger brother Jacob sought to deceive his aged father and obtain the blessing for himself. Unfortunately, Jacob's mother, Rebekah, conspired to succeed in deceiving Isaac. This episode reveals the importance of a father's blessing upon his son.

28:1, 3-4 In this reference we see the blessing passed on from Isaac to his son Jacob, "Isaac summoned Jacob, **blessed** him and commanded him: 'Don't take a wife from the Canaanite women.'" He told Jacob to return to their original home where he could find a wife. The spoken blessing was in the form of a **benediction:** "May God Almighty (El Shaddai) **bless** you and make you fruitful and multiply you, so that you become an assembly of peoples. May God give you and your offspring the **blessing** of Abraham, so that you may possess the land where you live as a foreigner, the land God gave to Abraham." Jacob was blessed by God in spite of his deceitfulness—showing His forgiving grace. Jacob's 12 sons became the 12 tribes of Israel, the foundation of an entire nation; all part of God's plan of redemption.

30:27, 30 Jacob remained in the family homeland until 11 of his sons were born. When he decided to return to the land of promise, his father-in-law Laban pleaded for him to stay, "If I have found favor in your sight, stay. I have learned by divination that the LORD has **blessed** me because of you. . . So Jacob replied, 'You know what I have done for you and your herds. For you had very little before I came, but now your wealth has increased. The Lord has **blessed** you because of me . . .'" Notice this testimony of God blessing one person because of someone else whom He chose to bless. Here we learn a significant truth: Yahweh often uses us as His channel of blessing to others.

31:48-49, 55 When the time came for Jacob to take his 11 sons and leave their homeland, his father-in-law Laban called for the making of a covenant, using stones as a monument to this solemn agreement. He said, "This mound is a witness between you and me today." The place was called "Mizpah" (which means "watch"). He then spoke this familiar **benediction**: "May the LORD watch between you and me when we are out of each other's sight . . . 'Laban got up early the next morning, kissed his grandchildren and daughters, and **blessed** them.'" Notice this father's act of blessing his family with a spoken benediction. There are times when I have followed this example in pronouncing a benediction upon my children and their families.

32:22-29 Here we find the episode of Jacob returning to meet his brother Esau who had every reason to hold a grudge against Jacob for stealing his birthright as well as their father's blessing. On the night before this dreaded encounter, Jacob had an amazing experience in which he literally wrestled with the Lord. When told to let go of this divine personage, Jacob said, "I will not let You go unless You **bless** me." At this point, the Lord told Jacob that his name would no longer be called Jacob (meaning "deceiver") but Israel (meaning "Prince with God"). The contest ends with these telling words, "And He **blessed** him there." One direct result of this blessing was a peaceful meeting with Esau the next day—a reunion in which Jacob gave his special gift (**blessing**) to Esau (33:11).

35:9 This reference is to a subsequent event in which God appeared to Jacob again, **blessing** him and repeating the change of his name to Israel.

39:5 Our study jumps across many years to the time when Joseph, the slave, had become an overseer in the house Pharaoh, the ruler of Egypt. The text makes this interesting observation: "From the time that he put him in charge of his household and of all that he owned, the LORD

9

blessed the Egyptian's house because of Joseph. LORD's **blessing** was on all that he owned, in his house and in his fields." How notable that Yahweh's blessing came to Joseph and through him to this pagan ruler and all his possessions. Likewise we will be blessed in order to be God's conduit of blessing to those around us—in our families, workplace, neighborhoods, and wherever we are.

47:7, 10 Years later Joseph brought his father, Jacob, to visit Pharaoh. On this auspicious occasion, we read, "Then Joseph brought his father Jacob and presented him before Pharaoh, and Jacob **blessed** Pharaoh." (See also verse 10.) Think of it. Here are two of the most influential people in the world in that day—Jacob, the patriarch of God's people, standing before Pharaoh, the sovereign ruler of the nation of Egypt; and what does Jacob do? He blessed Pharaoh! We aren't given his exact words, but they must have sounded strange to this pagan ruler. Surely God was in this unusual encounter, extending His blessing to the leader of the pagan world. Are we reaching out to the lost world around us with the blessings that have been given to us? "Pass it on."

48:3,9,15,16,20 The Book of Genesis concludes with the narrative of aged Jacob passing on to his family God's blessing on him. "God Almighty appeared to me at Luz in the land of Canaan and **blessed** me . . . bring them to me (his grandsons) and I will **bless** them . . . and he **blessed** Joseph, and said: 'The God before whom my fathers Abraham and Isaac walked, the God who has been my shepherd all my life to this day, the Angel who has redeemed me from all harm—may He **bless** these boys. And may they be called by my name and the names of my fathers Abraham and Isaac, and may they grow to be numerous within the land.'" Here is a blessing in the form of a **benediction**.

49:25,26,28 After prophesying the future for each of his sons, Jacob gave a final blessing to Joseph: "The God of your father who helps you, and by the Almighty who **blesses** you with **blessings** of heaven above, **blessings** of the deep that lies below, **blessings** of the breasts and of the womb. The **blessings** of your father excel the **blessings** of my ancestors . . . and he **blessed** them, and he **blessed** each one with a suitable **blessing**."

STUDY GUIDE

Prepare your responses to these questions and share them with other learners. (This same guide will occur at the end of each section—a total of twelve times.)

B Biblical Reference

Choose your favorite Scripture reference from this session and list it here. _____

Be prepared to explain your reason for this choice. _____

_____

L Learning

What new or helpful truth have you learned from this session?

_____

_____

E Example

Find an example from these biblical passages that expresses the manner in which you want to bless others. _____

_____

_____

S State

What blessing from God or from others have you received this week?

_____

_____

S Share

Tell about some way in which you recently blessed someone.

_____

_____

EXODUS

(Over 300 years after the close of Genesis)

Before Joseph died in Egypt at the age of 110 years, he told his brothers, "When God comes to your aid, you are to carry my bones up from here" (Gen. 50:25-26), meaning they were to bury him Canaan, the land God had promised them. However, it was actually 475 years later when his burial in Canaan took place (see Joshua 24:32).

Meanwhile the Israelites became enslaved by the Egyptians. The book of Exodus tells how God's people endured much suffering as slaves until He raised up Moses and Aaron to lead them out of their bondage. After a series of 10 plagues, Pharaoh, the ruler of Egypt, sent all the Israelites back to Canaan under Moses' leadership after 430 years (Ex. 12:40).

12:31-32 "He (Pharaoh) summoned Moses and Aaron during the night and said, 'Get up, leave my people, both you and the Israelites, and go worship Yahweh as you have asked. Take even your flocks and your herds as you have asked, and leave, and also **bless** me.' How interesting that this pagan ruler acknowledged Yahweh as God of these slaves, and asked that he receive a blessing from Moses and Aaron.

18:10 As Moses led his people out of Egypt on their way to the land God had promised them, they came to the area where Moses had served Jethro, the priest, his father-in-law as a shepherd. The text states, "Jethro rejoiced for all the good which the LORD had done for Israel, whom He had delivered out of the hand of the Egyptians. And Jethro said, 'Praise (**blessed**) be the LORD, who rescued you from Pharaoh and the power of the Egyptians . . . . Now I know that Yahweh is greater than all the gods . . .'" This priest also acknowledged Yahweh's sovereignty and spoke a word of blessing (praise) to Him.

20:11 Here is the list of the Ten Commandments, including the fourth command: "Remember the Sabbath day, to keep it holy . . . .Therefore the LORD **blessed** the Sabbath day and declared it holy."

23:23-25 God sent His people to occupy the promised land with these words: "My angel will go before you and bring you into the (promised land) . . . . So you shall worship the LORD your God, and He will **bless** your bread and your water. And I will remove illnesses from you." This promise of providing basic necessities during their long wilderness journey was literally fulfilled by the manna and water.

32:29 While Moses was on the mountain for forty days to receive the Ten Commandments and instructions for building the tabernacle, some of the Israelites became impatient and had Aaron make a golden calf for them to worship. When Moses came down and saw what they had done, he was extremely angry, breaking the tablets of stone, and calling for the destruction of all the idolaters (3,000 men). Then he said to the people, "Consecrate yourselves today to the LORD that He may bestow on you a **blessing** this day . . . ." (NKJV) The primary blessing needed by God's people at this time was forgiveness and cleansing from their sin.

39:43 After the people completed all the work for the tabernacle, "Then Moses inspected all the work they had accomplished. They had done just as the LORD commanded. Then Moses **blessed** them." The Book of Exodus closes with Moses pronouncing a blessing upon his people for all the good work of building a special place of worship, just as Yahweh had commanded them. Here is a reminder that Yahweh is well pleased when we seek to be obedient to His commands to us, and that He will also bless us.

LEVITICUS

(Covers one month of time)

Exodus concludes as the Israelites depart from Egypt and cross the Red Sea on their way to the area around Mt. Sinai. There Moses received many instructions regarding the Tabernacle, the priest's duties and garments, the Ten Commandments and other laws.

Leviticus, as the name implies, describes the work of the Levites who served as Israel's priests. The theme of this book is the holiness of Yahweh and how the people, through various offerings and feasts were to properly relate to their God.

9:22, 23 The focus of Leviticus is the commands of Yahweh regarding the proper times and ways to worship Him. Moses and Aaron were both descendants of Levi (thus Leviticus). The Levites were set apart to serve as worship leaders for God's people. In this passage Aaron fulfills his role in this manner: "Aaron lifted his hand toward the people, **blessed** them, and came down from offering the sin offering, the burnt offering, and peace offerings. And Moses and Aaron went into the tabernacle of meeting, and came out and **blessed** the people. Then the glory of the LORD appeared to all the people, and fire came out from before the LORD and consumed the burnt offering and the fat on the altar. When all the people saw it, they shouted and fell on their faces." Worship leaders today bless God's people as they lead in appropriate expressions of the offering of praise for our Lord Jesus making the ultimate and final sacrifice for sins, resulting in the peace of being in right relationship with Yahweh.

25:21 This chapter describes God's plans for His people to celebrate the Year of Jubilee, which was to be done each 50th year of their history. Every seventh year was to be a Sabbath year when no work was done, so after seven Sabbath years, the fiftieth year was another year of rest when there would be no work—no planting or harvesting. God anticipated the concern of His people when they would go two years of rest, how would they eat? His answer appears here: "And if you say, 'What shall we eat in the seventh year, (Year of Jubilee) since we shall not sow nor gather in our produce?' Then I will command My **blessing** on you in the sixth year, and it will bring forth produce enough for three years." What an amazing testimony of Yahweh's faithfulness to provide for all the needs of His people. His name is Yahweh Yireh ("I AM the One who provides for you.")

NUMBERS

(Begins one month after the close of Leviticus)

The Book of Numbers describes God's instructions to Moses to get the people organized for their journey to the land of promise. Also numerous laws are given regarding the duties of priests, offerings, and inheritances.

Consider one classic **benediction** and many occurrences of bless and blessing.

6:22-27 This passage gives what has become, without question, the best known and most often quoted **benediction** of the entire Old Testament.

"And the LORD spoke to Moses, saying, 'Speak to Aaron and his sons, saying," This is the way you shall **bless** the children of Israel. Say to them:

> **May Yahweh bless you and protect you;**
>
> **may Yahweh make His face shine on you,**
>
> **and be gracious to you.**
>
> **may Yahweh look with favor on you,**
>
> **and give you peace.**

"So they shall put My name on the children of Israel and I will **bless** them."

Here is an excellent **benediction** for us to use in offering the LORD'S blessing to others. I have often shared this blessing with others— sometimes to telephone solicitation calls, or to those delivering goods to our house, etc.

Peter Christian Lutkin (1858-1931) Dean of Music at Northwestern University in Evanston, Illinois, composed a **benediction** for his church choir that is familiar to most Christians today. You may remember these words:

The Lord bless you and keep you; The Lord lift up His countenance upon you, and give you peace, and give you peace."

Notice the term "peace" at the conclusion of this benediction. "Peace" is the Hebrew word "shalom," a very special term meaning harmony, prosperity, wholeness, completeness, welfare, and tranquility. When Hebrew people greet one another today, they say, "Shalom Aleichem," meaning, "Peace to you." The other person replies, "Aleichem Shalom," meaning, "And peace to you also."

22:6-24:10 There are some eight references to "bless" and "blessing" in this passage. All these refer to the actions of Balaam, a prophet, who was asked by Balak, the king of the Moabites, to speak a curse on his enemies, the Israelites. Instead Balaam was told by God to bless His people, which he did. Thus another example of Yahweh's determined favor upon His chosen ones.

DEUTERONOMY

The term "Deuteronomy" means second law; it is the record of the final three messages Moses gave his people just before they crossed the Jordan River to conquer the land promised to them by Yahweh. There are about 45 occurrences of the word "bless" or "blessed" in this last book of the Pentateuch (first five books of the Bible). Moses gave a brief summary of the past 40 years when Israel made their way from bondage in Egypt to the banks of the Jordan River; he reminded them of the numerous ways in which Yahweh had blessed them throughout their journey. Now we will examine most of these references.

1:11 This first reference includes a **benediction** that Moses gave his people. "May Yahweh, the God of your fathers increase you a thousand more, and **bless** you as He promised you." At this time Israel numbered several million persons, and Moses claimed their multiplication, which ultimately came to pass.

2:7 "For the LORD your God has **blessed** you in all the work of your hands. . . . The LORD your God has been with you this past forty years, and you have lacked nothing." Moses reminded his people of their forty year pilgrimage during which nothing they needed was lacking—because Yahweh was with them. The same is true of our journey through this life—He is with us; we have everything we need.

7:13-14 After reminding the people of the Ten Commandments (chapter 5) and the Great Commandment (chapter 6), Moses declared that if his people would keep these commands, "He will love you, and **bless** you, and multiply you. He will **bless** your descendants, and the produce of your land . . . . You will be **blessed** above all peoples." Yahweh's promise to bless was conditional—His people must obey His laws. Today, under grace, we are given unconditional promises of blessing.

8:10 Now Moses looks to the future, when Israel has moved into the land of promise. "When you eat and are full, you shall praise (**bless)** the LORD your God for the good land which He has given you." By faith Moses knew what the future held for these Israelites; he cautioned them not to forget the Giver of all their blessings.

10:8 Looking back to God's choice of the tribe of Levi to be Israel's priests, Moses referred to their role: "At that time the LORD separated the tribe of Levi to bear the ark of the LORD's covenant, to stand before Yahweh to serve Him, and to pronounce **blessings** in His name as it is today." An important aspect of their task was to declare Yahweh's blessing upon His people (see Numbers 6:22-27, the Aaronic blessing).

11:26-29; 30:1, 16-19 These verses give a summary of the choice Yahweh gave His people: "Look, today I set before you a **blessing** and a curse: there will be a **blessing** if you obey the commands of the LORD your God. I am giving you today you today, and a curse if you do not obey the commands of the LORD your God. . . . When the LORD your God brings you into the land you are entering to possess, you are to proclaim the blessing at Mount Gerizim and the curse at Mount Ebal." Notice the designation of Gerizim as the mount of blessing and Ebal as the mount of the curse. People were free to choose the way of God's blessing by choosing to obey His commands. Unfortunately, there were many times when they made the wrong choice, and suffered the consequences.

Here is a list of many other references to "bless" and "blessing" in Deuteronomy. These relate to many subjects such as the proper place of worship, tithing and principles of giving, the role of priests, and other practical manners all of which Yahweh promises His blessing: 12:7, 15 ; 14:24, 29; 15:4-18; 16:10-17; 21:5; 23:20; 24:13, 19; 26:15; 29:12; 28: 2-18 (9 times); 29:19.

33:11-24. Moses records his final blessings, "This is the **blessing** that Moses, the man of God, **blessed** the children of Israel before his death." Each of the 12 tribes are mentioned with a specific blessing. One is most notable: "And of Asher he said: 'Asher be the most **blessed** of the sons. May he be the most favored among his brothers, and let him dip his foot in olive oil. May the bolts of your gate be iron and bronze, and your strength last as long as you live. . . . The God of old is your dwelling place, and underneath are the everlasting arms'" (vv. 24-27). It is interesting that this long chapter describing Yahweh's blessing, follows an even longer account (chapter 32) of the Song of Moses, in which he describes the judgment of God which will surely come upon Israel due to their unfaithfulness to God's covenant with them. In spite of knowing Israel's future failure to keep His commands, Yahweh promises His blessings. What a powerful revelation of love and grace!

(Moses is the only person in the Old Testament to be described as "the man of God," (33:1); he also is the only person whom God buried.) (34:6).

STUDY GUIDE

Prepare your responses to these questions and share them with other learners.

B Biblical Reference

Choose your favorite Scripture reference from this session and list it here. _____

Be prepared to explain your reason for this choice. _____

_____

L Learning

What new or helpful truth have you learned from this session?

_____

_____

E Example

Find an example from these biblical passages that expresses the manner in which you want to bless others. _____

_____

_____

S State

What blessing from God or from others have you received this week?

_____

_____

S Share

Tell about some way in which you recently blessed someone.

_____

_____

JOSHUA

Joshua was God's choice to succeed Moses as the leader of His people. His name means "Yahweh is salvation," and is the Hebrew equivalent of the Greek name "Jesus." The time for this record of Israel's conquest of the land of promise is around 1250 B.C. and covers about 25 years. Joshua was the first-born son of Nun; only he and Caleb, out of some 3 million who left Egypt, survived the 40 years of wilderness wandering and entered Canaan. We will examine the eight references to "bless" and "blessing" in his book.

8:34 After Joshua led the Israelites in conquering the first two cities in Canaan, Jericho and Ai, he built an altar to Yahweh on Mount Ebal. Then he gathered the people before the ark of the LORD and the priests were ordered to proclaim a blessing upon them. (See Deuteronomy 27.) "Afterward Joshua read aloud all the words of the law-- the **blessings** as well as the curses-- according to all that is written in the book of the Law." Joshua obeyed the command of Moses to remind the people of God's promise to bless them or curse them according to their response to His word. All this reminds us that we also have a choice regarding His word to us; we can choose to obey or not, then be blessed or suffer consequences for our disobedience.

14:13; 15:19 These verses speak of Caleb who was the only Israelite, along with Joshua, who agreed to claim the land of promise when the first spies surveyed the land. Now, some 45 years later, he asked Joshua to give him and his family the land promised him by Moses. "Then Joshua **blessed** Caleb son of Jephunneh and gave him Hebron as an inheritance." Later (15:19) Caleb's daughter, Achsah, asked him to give her a field. She said to him, "Give me a **blessing. S**ince you have given me land in the Negev, give me also springs of water also. So he gave her the upper and lower springs." Sometimes God's blessings are delayed, but they always come.

17:14 "Then the children of Joseph (Manasseh and Ephraim) spoke to Joshua saying, 'Why did you give us only one tribal allotment as an inheritance? We have many people, because the LORD has been **blessing** us greatly."' Joshua replied to this request by offering them a larger portion, but they were unable to claim it.

22:6-7, 33 "Joshua **blessed** them and sent them on their way, and they went to their homes. . . . When Joshua sent them away to their homes, he **blessed** them.

This chapter gives the account of those Israelites, (Reubenites, Gadites, and half the tribe of Manasseh,) who, with Moses' permission, claimed their inheritance of land on the east side of Jordan. After first helping their kinsmen conquer Canaan, they were blessed by Joshua for this assistance, then permitted to claim their preferred land. Later, when they built an altar as a reminder to their descendants, this action was perceived by their kinsmen as being an expression of rebellion against the LORD (v. 19), however, when they explained their true motive, the two sides had peace. "So the thing pleased the children of Israel, and the children of Israel praised (**blessed**) God, they spoke no more of going against them in battle, to destroy the land where the children of Reuben and Gad dwelt." Here is an example of how a misunderstanding led to a serious division among God's people. But when the two sides explained their differences, peace and blessing prevailed. Good lesson here for us today.

24:10 "But I would not listen to Balaam. Instead, he repeatedly **blessed** you. And I delivered you from his hand."

The final reference to bless is part of a lengthy recap of the history of Israel from God's call to Abraham all the way to their present. Included, is the account of the prophet Balaam refusing to curse Israel, choosing rather to bless them as God led him to do.

The clear testimony of all the book of Joshua is that Israel was Yahweh's chosen people, whom He consistently blessed by promising them a special land, and enabling them to conquer and settle in that land.

JUDGES

Following the death of Joshua, came a period when Israel lacked strong leadership, the kind of leaders like Joshua who were committed to keeping Yahweh's commands. For a period of about 325 years God's people went through a series of cycles described by sin, suffering, supplication, and salvation. Two areas of disobedience caused this long era of national trouble: (1) failure to destroy the pagan inhabitants of Canaan, and (2) intermarriage with these people which led to the worship of their false gods.

In His mercy God continued to bless His people by sending them a series of 12 judges in hopes of delivering them from their sinful ways. These men and women acted as spiritual leaders, but none were successful. Here are the brief references to "bless" and "blessing."

1:15 The story from Joshua 15:19 is repeated here as Caleb's daughter, Achsah, asks him to give her a **blessing**—in terms of springs of water for her land.

5:2, 9 One of the 12 judges was a woman named Deborah. In this passage we read of her song which says, "When leaders lead in Israel, when the people volunteer, praise (**bless**) the LORD. . . . My heart is with the rulers of Israel, with the volunteers of the people. Praise (**Bless**) the LORD." Deborah was giving praise to Yahweh for leaders who willingly gave themselves to honor Him. We should follow that worthy example today.

5:24-27 Deborah continues her song by recounting the deed of another woman: "Jael is most **blessed** of women, the wife of Heber the Kenite; she is most **blessed** among tent-dwelling women." The occasion for these words of praise is the manner in which Jael murdered Sisera, the commander of the enemy's army—by driving a tent peg through his skull! Certainly not an example for us to follow.

13:24-25 More information in the Book of Judges is given to Samson than to any of the other judges. Here his birth is described, "So the woman gave birth to a son and named him Samson. The boy grew, and the LORD **blessed** him." There are four times when this phrase is repeated, indicating how the LORD blessed him: "And the Spirit of the LORD began to direct him . . . ." (13:25; 14:6, 19; 15:14). The amazing feats of strength which Samson performed were all due to this special blessing of Yahweh. He will bless us with the strength to do His will.

17:2 This final reference to "blessing" gives a brief account of a mother's benediction to her son, "My son, you are **blessed** by the LORD." These are beautiful words, however, this son, Micah, went on to create a shrine to an idol rather than to honor Yahweh. And this confirms the sad commentary on God's people which occurs at the end of this book: "In those days there was no king in Israel; everyone did what he wanted." (21:25). Sad state of affairs.

18:6 "The priest told them, 'Go in peace. the LORD is watching over the journey you are going on.'"

This **<u>benediction</u>** was spoken by a young priest as he sent five men from the tribe of Dan on their journey.

The clear message of Judges is that Yahweh is faithful to bless His people even when they choose to go astray from Him. He continues to send chosen leaders to call them back to Himself when they are wayward. Sometimes His blessings come in the form of chastisement, but always for the salvation of His people.

RUTH

This lovely story occurred during the time of the Judges and clearly reveals the sovereignty of Yahweh, ruling over the affairs of His people. In spite of the troublesome times, including a famine in the land of promise, God worked out His purposes. [Only two Bible books are named for women: Ruth and Esther; only the book of Ruth is all about a woman.]

In review, Yahweh began His redemptive plan by calling Abram to be the first of His chosen people and the first to know of the special land He promised for them to live. Next, He called Moses and Joshua to lead His people in claiming their appointed land. Now, in the marriage of Boaz and Ruth, a family line began through which the Savior would be born. All these happened in keeping with Yahweh's sovereign purpose of providing salvation for all nations. Note the five references of "bless" and "blessing" in the book of Ruth.

1:8-9 Although these terms do not occur here, we have a clear statement of a beautiful **benediction**: "And Naomi said to her two daughters-in-law, 'Each of you go back to your mother's home. May the LORD show faithful love to you [chesed] as you have shown to the dead and to me. May the LORD enable each of you to find security in the house of your new husband.'" Naomi was willing to release the wives of her dead sons that they might begin new families—with her blessing and the blessing of Yahweh. Certainly a gracious act on her part.

2:4 "Later when Boaz arrived from Bethlehem, he said to the harvesters, 'The LORD be with you! The LORD **bless you** they replied'" These typical words of greeting reveal the good relationship Boaz had with his field workers. Even today, we may well share this kind of blessing in greeting others.

2:12 A second **benediction** is found in these words which Boaz spoke to Ruth when he first met her, learning of her loyalty to Naomi her mother-in-law, "May the LORD reward you for what you have done, and may you receive a full reward from the LORD God of Israel, under whose wings you have come for refuge." His blessing reveals an unusual kindness toward a Moabite widow. Jews traditionally had no dealings with outsiders like Ruth. Are we as hospitable toward "outsiders" in our midst?

2:19-20 When Ruth returned home after a day of gleaning in the fields of Boaz, Naomi inquired about her work, "Where did you gather barley today, and where did you work? May the LORD **bless** the man who noticed you." So Ruth told her, "The name of the man I worked with today is Boaz." "Then Naomi said to her daughter-in-law, 'May he be **blessed** by the LORD, who has not forsaken His kindness to the living or the dead!' "And Naomi said to her, 'The man is a close relative. He is one of our family redeemers.'" How interesting, and how revealing of God's providence is this remarkable happening. Of all the fields where Ruth might have chosen to work, she was obviously led by Yahweh to choose the field of Boaz.

3:10 Later, Naomi advised Ruth regarding the proper procedure for offering herself to Boaz. After lying at his feet and introducing herself to Boaz, he said to Ruth, "May the LORD **bless you,** my daughter. You have shown more kindness now than before, because have not pursued younger men, whether rich or poor. Now, do not be afraid, my daughter. I will do for you all whatever you say, since all the people of my town know that you are a woman of noble character." Even though Ruth was a foreigner, she had gained an outstanding reputation among her new associates; they all admired her for her kindness to Naomi.

4:11-12 When Boaz publicly announced that he was fulfilling his responsibility to Naomi as a near-kinsman, he promised to raise up children to her deceased husband and likewise to her two sons, by marrying Ruth. All the people offered this **benediction** to him: "May the LORD make the woman who is entering your house like Rachel and Leah, who together built the house of Israel. May you be powerful in Ephrathah and famous in Bethlehem. May your house be like the house of Perez, the son Tamar bore to Judah, because of the offspring the LORD will give you from this young woman." (Boaz was a direct descendant of Perez.)

4:14 Later Boaz and Ruth were blessed with a son, Obed, who became the father of Jesse, David's father. After the birth of Obed, the women said to Naomi, "Praise (**Blessed**) be the LORD, who has not left you without a family redeemer today. May his name become well known in Israel. He will renew your life and sustain you in your old age. Indeed, your daughter-in-law, who loves you and is better to you than seven sons, has given birth to him." (Here is the only biblical reference to one woman loving another.)

How interesting that Boaz was the son of Rahab, the harlot of Jericho. So here are two non-Jewish women, Rahab and Ruth, who were an important part of the family tree of Jesus. According to the genealogy of Jesus in Matthew 1, His father Joseph was a direct descendent of David.

Thus this little biblical narrative speaks volumes to us regarding Yahweh's sovereignty over what seem like ordinary human events. He foresaw the ultimate birth of His Son and arranged the characters who were needed for this saving event to occur.

STUDY GUIDE

Prepare your responses to these questions and share them with other learners.

B Biblical Reference

Choose your favorite Scripture reference from this session and list it here. _____

Be prepared to explain your reason for this choice. _____

_____

L Learning

What new or helpful truth have you learned from this session?

_____

_____

E Example

Find an example from these biblical passages that expresses the manner in which you want to bless others. _____

_____

_____

S State

What blessing from God or from others have you received this week?

_____

_____

S Share

Tell about some way in which you recently blessed someone.

_____

_____

FIRST AND SECOND SAMUEL

The books of First and Second Samuel mark a significant change in Israel's history. Samuel was the last of the judges and the first of the prophets. During his time, Israel went from a theocracy (direct rule of God) to a monarchy (the rule of kings). Three men are most influential during this time (1105-970 B.C.): Samuel who founded the school of the prophets, Saul, the first of the kings, and David, the greatest of the kings. For the purpose of our study, we find over 20 references to bless and blessings here, plus four benedictions.

First Samuel covers about 115 years, from the birth of Samuel till the death of King Saul.

First Samuel 1:17 "Then Eli answered and said, 'Go in peace, and may the God of Israel grant the petition you've requested from Him.'" Eli the priest pronounced this **benediction** upon Hannah, the mother-to-be of Samuel, as she prayed in the temple.

2:20 Samuel's parents gave him to serve the Lord under the guidance of Eli, the priest. Each year when they came to visit him, "Eli would **bless** Elkanah and his wife: 'May the LORD give you children by this woman in place of the one she has given to the LORD.'. . . The LORD paid attention to Hannah's need, and she conceived and gave birth to three sons and two daughters." These words of Eli form a **benediction** that proved to be very effective because before this blessing, Hannah had been barren. Here is a fine example of how Yahweh rewards our gifts to Him, often more abundantly than our gifts.

9:13 On a day when Samuel was to offer a sacrifice to the LORD, the people were awaiting his arrival. "The people won't eat (the sacrifice) until he (Samuel) comes, because he must **bless** the sacrifice." (This may be the background of our practice of asking someone to "bless the food" before we eat it.)

15:13 Much later, Samuel became a respected judge in Israel, however, his sons proved to be unworthy to succeed him. So the people asked for a king to lead them, just as other nations had. In spite of his warning to the people, they insisted on having a king. Yahweh instructed Samuel to anoint Saul to be king. Saul started his reign well but later proved to be a poor choice. On this occasion (15:13) he pretended to have obeyed the LORD but actually disobeyed. Upon seeing Samuel he said, "May the LORD **bless** you. I have carried out the LORD's instructions." The prophet knew better and announced that God had rejected Saul from being king. One lesson here for us is the danger of covering our disobedience by casually declaring God's blessing upon others. We cannot offer His blessing when we are being unfaithful to Him.

23:21 The Ziphites were a family group among the tribe of Judah where David took refuge from King Saul. When they offered to deliver David to Saul, he said to them, "May you be **blessed** by the LORD, for you have taken pity on me." Here is a rare example of attributing God's blessing falsely; He would never bless the enemies of His chosen servant.

25:32-33, 39. Here is the story of how a woman named Abigal prevented David from an injustice against Nabal, her husband. When David realized how she had intervened, he said to her, "Praise **(blessed)** be the LORD God of Israel, who sent you to meet me today! Your discernment is **blessed** and you are **blessed**. Today you kept me from participating in bloodshed and avenging myself by my own hand." Later David heard of Nabal's death. "When David heard that Nabal was dead, he said, 'Praise **(blessed)** be the LORD, who championed my cause against Nabal's insults and restrained His servant from doing evil.'" Then David took Abigail to be his wife. David was humble enough to recognize the wisdom of this woman and that she was sent by Yahweh to bless him. We learn from this the possibility of God sending unlikely persons to bless us with wise counsel.

26:25 King Saul pursued David with the intent to kill him. On this occasion David withheld his own hand from killing the king. As a result, Saul repented of his evil plan and gave David this **benediction**, "You are **blessed** my son David! You shall certainly do great things and will also prevail." We see in this episode the protective hand of God upon His chosen servant.

Second Samuel begins with the death of King Saul and focuses on the forty-year reign of David as Israel's best king.

Second Samuel 2:5 The first of 14 references to bless in 2 Samuel concerns King David's **benediction** to those men who buried Saul: "The LORD **bless** you, because you have shown this kindness to Saul your lord when you buried him. And now may the LORD show kindness and faithfulness to you." This was David's first action following his being anointed as king over Judah. This is a good indication of the gracious attitude of this new king over God's people.

6:11-12, 18, 20 After David became king over both Juda and Israel, he decided to bring the Ark of the Covenant to Jerusalem. However, for three months on the way to Jerusalem, the ark was kept in the home of Obed –edom. We read, "The LORD **blessed** Obed-edom and his whole family." It was reported to David: "7The LORD **blessed** Obed-edom's family and all and all that belongs to him because of the ark of God." When David heard about this, he had the ark moved to Jerusalem. There the king had animal sacrifices to be made, and "he **blessed** the people in the name of Yahweh of Hosts." Later, David "returned home to **bless** his household." We learn from these accounts how important this practice of blessing people was to King David. Likewise, we should follow this biblical example.

7:29 David's lengthy prayer of thanksgiving for all Yahweh's goodness to him concludes with these impressive words, "Now, O Lord God, You are God, and Your words are true, and You have promised this goodness to Your servant. Now therefore, let it please You to **bless** the house of Your servant, that it may continue forever before You; for You O Lord God, have spoken it, and with Your **blessing** let the house of Your servant be **blessed** forever." Again, note the repeated use of the term "bless" or "blessed" indicating David's awareness of the importance of this expression of Yahweh's favor.

8:10, 13:25, 18:28, 19:39, 21:3 Here is a series of references to one person **blessing** another. These show us the importance of speaking words of favor to encourage one another.

22:47 David composed many songs during his lifetime. His final song is found in chapter 22. One notable phrase from this song is found in verse 47: "The LORD lives! **Blessed** be my Rock! Let God be exalted, the Rock of my salvation." In the final chapter of 2 Samuel, David declares of Yahweh, "He has made with me an everlasting covenant" (23:5).

Before leaving the biblical record of David, let us review Yahweh's major prophecies regarding His covenants with His people. First, in Genesis 3:15 we are told that the seed of the woman (ultimately Jesus) would bruise the head of the serpent (Satan). This is God's promise to the human **race**. Second, a promise to **one nation**, to Abraham in Genesis 22:18, "In thy seed shall all the nations of the earth be blessed." The third was made to **one tribe** in that race, to Jacob in Genesis 49:10, "The scepter shall not depart from Judah . . . until Shiloh come." And finally, in 2 Samuel 7:16, to **one family** in that tribe, these words from Yahweh to David, "Your house and your kingdom shall be established forever before you. Your throne shall be established forever." All these promises reveal God's plan to provide salvation for all people through His Son, our Lord Jesus. *Here is the greatest of all His blessings!*

FIRST AND SECOND KINGS

These books originally were one document covering about 400 years, from the death of David, followed by the reign of Solomon, until the division and captivity of Israel and Judah. Also featured in 2 Kings is the ministry of the prophets Elijah and Elisha. We will consider 9 references to bless and blessing, plus one benediction here.

First Kings 1:47-48 King David was nearing death when one of his servants said, "Solomon has even taken his seat on the royal throne. The king's servants have also gone to congratulate (**bless**) our lord King David saying, 'May your God make the name of Solomon more well known than your name, and may He make his throne greater than your throne.' "Then the king bowed himself on the bed. Also the king said thus '**Blessed** be the LORD God of Israel, who has given one to sit on my throne this day, while my eyes see it!'" These words of blessing and **benediction** reveal the gracious spirit of David as he celebrated the anointing of his son Solomon to be his successor. Note the lack of any sense of envy or resentment on David's part; rather, he celebrated and blessed Yahweh for Solomon being recognized as king.

2:45 These are the words of Solomon concerning his reign as king: "But King Solomon will be **blessed** and David's throne will remain established before the LORD forever." Solomon had an awareness that his position as king was the direct result of Yahweh's blessing, not his own achievement. Likewise, whatever status we may gain is always and totally God's gift to us.

5:7 Hiram, king of Tyre, became the friend of Solomon and provided cedar trees for the construction of Solomon's temple in Jerusalem. He said, "May the LORD be praised (**blessed**) today! He has given David a wise son over this great people." Here was a pagan ruler who recognized Yahweh's appointment of Solomon and praised Him for this blessing. Hopefully, our reputation among those outside of God's family will see in us Yahweh's favor.

8:14-15, 56-61, 66. The most noteworthy achievement of King Solomon was the construction of the temple in Jerusalem. On the momentous occasion of the dedication of this magnificent structure, we read of Solomon's speech and his lengthy prayer. First, "he **blessed** the whole congregation of Israel, while all the congregation of Israel was standing. Then he said: '**Blessed** be the LORD God of Israel, who spoke with His mouth to my father David, and with His hand has fulfilled. . .His word.'" Then, following a very beautiful prayer, he proceeded to offer this blessing and **benediction**: "He stood and **blessed** all the congregation of Israel with a loud voice saying, '**Blessed** be the LORD, who has given rest to His people Israel according to all the He promised. . . May the LORD our God be with us. . .May He not leave us nor forsake us, that He may incline our heart to Himself.'" (There are a total of six occurrences of "may" to express this very meaningful **benediction.**) "On the eighth day he sent the people away; and they **blessed** the king, and went to their tents joyful and glad of heart for all the goodness that the LORD had done for His servant David, and for Israel His people."

10:9 Later the queen of Sheba came to see all the achievements of Solomon and to listen to his words of wisdom. In response she declared, "**Blessed** be the LORD your God, who delighted in you, setting you on the throne of Israel. Because the LORD has loved Israel forever, therefore He made you king, to do justice and righteousness." Thus another pagan ruler offered a tribute of blessing to Yahweh when she beheld all the amazing things He had done.

Second Kings 5:15 This single reference to a blessing is the occasion when Naaman, the commander of the army of Syria, came to the prophet Elisha. He had heard of this prophet's power to work miracles and hoped to be cured of his leprosy. After obeying Elisha's command to dip himself seven times in the Jordan River, he was completely healed, and said, "Indeed, now I know that there is no God in all the earth except in Israel; now, therefore please take a gift (**blessing**) from your servant." [Some translations render the Hebrew term berekah as "gift," others as "blessing."] Again, here is a pagan leader who becomes convinced of the fact that Yahweh is the only true God. His goodness to this man opened his eyes to ultimate truth.

Comment on the Biblical Concept of Yahweh's Blessings

Most of the references to blessings we have studied thus far reveal Yahweh's favor toward His chosen people. He takes the initiative in reaching out to sinful persons with His kindness, working through human experiences to bring about good results. Consider one familiar statement of this fact from the pen of the apostle Paul"

"We know that God works all things together for the good of those who love God and are called according to His purpose" (Romans 8:28).

33

Consider these comforting words of truth from a man who suffered a severe stroke.

"THIS I KNOW"

There is nothing—no circumstance, no trouble, no testing that can ever touch me until--

First of all, it has come past God and past Christ, right through to me. And if it has come that far, it has come with a great purpose which I may not understand at the moment. But as I refuse to become panicky, as I lift up my eyes to Him and accept it as coming from the throne of God for some great purpose of **blessing** for my own heart; no sorrow will ever disturb me, no trial will ever disarm me, no circumstance will ever cause me to fret—for I shall rest in the joy of who my Lord is!

-- Alan Redpath

STUDY GUIDE

Prepare your responses to these questions and share them with other learners.

B Biblical Reference

Choose your favorite Scripture reference from this session and list it here. _____

Be prepared to explain your reason for this choice. _____

_____

L Learning

What new or helpful truth have you learned from this session?

_____

_____

E Example

Find an example from these biblical passages that expresses the manner in which you want to bless others. _____

_____

_____

S State

What blessing from God or from others have you received this week?

_____

_____

S Share

Tell about some way in which you recently blessed someone.

_____

_____

FIRST AND SECOND CHRONICLES

As is true for the books of Samuel and Kings, the Chronicles (histories) were originally one volume. And they cover the same basic materiel found in the books of Samuel and Kings—a recap of this same history with some added information—to the end of the Jews' exile in Babylon and return to Judea in 538 B.C. However, the purpose of the Chronicles is different than the Samuel and Kings books; while they follow the path of an historical record, Chronicles (probably written by Ezra) traces the fact of Yahweh's choice of one family to be His agents of salvation and one temple in one city to be His focal point in that saving provision for all humankind. For the purpose of our study we now focus on all references to blessings and benedictions in these two books.

First Chronicles 4:10 This reference became rather popular several years ago and was widely featured as "The Prayer of Jabez." Here are the words of his prayer, "If only You would **bless** me, extend my border, let Your hand be with me, and keep me from harm, so that I will not cause any pain!" (The name Jabez literally means "He will cause pain.") The verse goes on to state: "And God granted his request." Certainly all these are legitimate requests, however, the focus of this prayer is rather selfish—here is what I want You to do for me! As we noted in the beginning of our study, Yahweh wants to bless us in order to make us a blessing to Him and to others.

12:18 This **benediction** was inspired by the Holy Spirit who came upon Amasai who said to King David, "We are yours, O David, We are on your side, O son of Jesse! Peace, peace to you, and peace to your helpers! For your God helps you." Three times the term peace ("shalom") appears in this spoken blessing.

13:14 (Same event as recorded in 2 Samuel 6:12.)

16:2, 36 When David brought the ark of God to Jerusalem and placed it in the tabernacle (tent), he led in offerings to God and "he **blessed** the people in the name of Yahweh." Later he composed a lengthy song to celebrate this event, saying, "May Yahweh, the God of Israel be praised (**blessed**) from everlasting to everlasting." (16:36) So he first blessed the people, then Yahweh for this momentous occasion of placing the ark, symbolizing Yahweh's presence, among His people. Likewise, we celebrate His continuous presence among us and within us!

17:27 Chapter 17 records God's covenant with David, assuring him of His unending favor upon him and His chosen people. In response David declared, "You have been pleased to **bless** the house of Your servant, that it may continue before You forever; for You have **blessed** it, O LORD, and it shall be **blessed** forever." Note the repetition of "bless" and "blessed," indicating this king's awareness that all his prominence and prosperity is due then and forever to Yahweh's favor. We are the benefactors today of this covenant of blessing.

23:13 As David neared the end of his life, he made certain that the Levites would continue their appointed task of leading the worship of Yahweh's people. This text states that, "Aaron was set apart, he and his sons forever, that he should consecrate the most holy things, to burn incense in the presence of Yahweh, to minister to Him and to pronounce b**lessings** in His name forever." Aaron and his family were the descendants of Levi. Their assignment was to perform the various aspects of worship along with declaring God's spoken blessing, first recorded in Numbers 6:22-27. One of David's final acts was to ensure that this procedure would continue.

26:5 Earlier (13:14) we read of God's blessing upon Obed-Edom, here the same blessing continues upon his eighth son, Peullethai, "for God **blessed** him." How interesting to see the favor of God from one generation to the next. May this be so among us and our descendants.

29:10-11, 20 Chapter 29 recounts all the preparations David made for the construction of the temple in Jerusalem. After the people brought an abundance of materials, we read this final **benediction** from David, "May You be praised (**blessed**) LORD God of our father Israel, forever and ever. Yours, O LORD is the greatness, the power, and the glory, the victory, and the majesty; for all that is in heaven and in earth is Yours. . . Then

David said to all the congregation, 'Now **bless** the LORD your God.' So all the congregation **blessed** the LORD God of their fathers, and bowed their heads and prostrated themselves before the LORD and the king." All these references to blessing the LORD refer to the offering of praise and thanksgiving to Him—all expressions of worship and adoration. Certainly, our worship today should be focused on similar ways of blessing Him.

Second Chronicles This presents the history of Judah beginning with King Solomon and including the decree of the Persian ruler Cyrus for all Jews to return from Babylonian captivity to their home in Palestine, a period totaling about 440 years.

2:12 These are the words of Hiram, King of Tyre, (1 Kings 5:7) who provided much of the materials for building Solomon's temple in Jerusalem: "**Blessed** be the LORD God of Israel, who made heaven and earth, for He has given King David a wise son . . . who will build a temple for the LORD and a royal house for himself!"

[Chapters 3-7 describe the building and dedication of Solomon's temple (959 B.C.) This was his crowning achievement, symbolizing God's presence among His people. This impressive structure stood until it was destroyed by the Babylonians in 586 B.C.]

6:3-4 (Same as 1 Kings 8:14-15; Solomon blessing his people.)

9:8 (Same as 1 Kings 10:9; Queen of Sheba blessing Yahweh.)

20:26 Here is a most interesting location in our study; a place named **The Valley of Berachah** (**blessing**). God's people gained an impressive victory over their enemies here—so great that it took three days for them to carry away all the loot. "On the fourth day they assembled in the Valley of Berachah, for there they **blessed** the LORD; the name of that place was called, The Valley of Berachah until this day." There is a true sense in which we live in The Valley of Berachah today—the place of Yahweh's blessing, today and every day.

30:18-19, 26-27   King Hezekiah called for a nation-wide observance of the Passover. However, some of the people were not ceremonially clean for this sacred event. Therefore the king offered this **benediction**: "May the good LORD provide atonement for everyone who prepares his heart on seeking Yahweh, the God of his ancestors, though he is not cleansed according to the purification of the sanctuary. And the LORD listened to Hezekiah and healed the people." Then the people observed the Feast of Unleavened Bread for fourteen days, offering thousands of sacrificed animals. "So there was great joy in Jerusalem, for since the time of Solomon, the son of David, king of Israel, there had been nothing like this in Jerusalem. Then the priests, the Levites, arose and **blessed** the people, and their voice was heard, and their prayer came up to His holy dwelling place, to heaven." What a remarkable time of worship and dedication to Yahweh.

31:8, 10 King Hezekiah continued his reforms by having all pagan altars destroyed. Then he called for the people to bring tithes and offerings for the support of the priests; so great was the response that there were literally heaps of goods; the text reports: "When Hezekiah and the leaders came and saw the heaps, they **blessed** the LORD and His people Israel. . . the LORD has **blessed** His people and what is left is this great abundance." Note the two expressions of "blessed"—the people blessed the LORD by their gifts of tithes and offerings; then the LORD blessed the people for their generosity. What we see happening is the kind of prosperity Yahweh desires for His people—and will provide when they determine to be faithful as His stewards through their tithes and offerings.

However, due to the unfaithfulness of His people, chapter 36 records the fall of Jerusalem in 586 B.C. followed by the Babylonian Captivity. Second Chronicles ends with the story of God restoring His people to Jerusalem by the degree of Cyrus, the king of Persia in 538 B.C.

THE HISTORY OF SOLOMON'S TEMPLE IN JERUSALEM

The temple represented the presence of Yahweh. Solomon built the first temple which was dedicated in 959 B.C. That structure remained until it was destroyed by the Babylonians in 586 B.C. When the first group of exiles returned from captivity in Babylon, they rebuilt the temple in 516 B.C. seventy years later, just as the prophets predicted. This second temple remained until A.D. 70 when the Romans destroyed it.

Temple dedication	Solomon	2 Chronicles 5:1	ca. 959 B.C.
First repair and reform	Asa	" 15:8	ca. 895 B.C.
Second repair and reform	Joash	" 24:13	ca 830 B.C.
Third repair and reform	Hezekiah	" 29:3	ca 715 B.C.
Fourth repair and reform	Josiah	" 34:8	ca 622 B.C.
Temple destruction	Zedekiah	" 36:19	ca 586 B.C.
Temple rebuilt	Zerubbabel	Ezra 3-4	516 B.C.
Temple repaired	King Herod	The New Testament era	20 B.C.
Temple destroyed by Romans			A.D. 70

These events are included here due to the fact that, beginning with the Tabernacle in the wilderness, and continuing with the temples in Jerusalem, all are evidence of Yahweh's blessing upon His chosen people. However, since the outpouring of God's Spirit upon His church (Acts 2), believers have become His temples; He now lives in us, not in some material structure. Unlike previous times when Yahweh came upon chosen leaders for a temporary empowerment or ability, He now resides permanently by His Spirit in every believer; this is the greatest of all His blessings!

EZRA

Originally the books of Ezra and Nehemiah were one. The book of Ezra describes two restorations of the Hebrew captives in Babylon. First, more than 40,000 captives returned under the leadership of Sheshbazzar (1:8) and began rebuilding the temple in Jerusalem (530s B.C.) Second, Ezra led a smaller group to return about 458 B.C. His purpose was to teach people Yahweh's law and restore temple worship. Consider the single occurrence of the word blessed in this book.

7:27-28 Artaxerxes was the king of Persia when Ezra, the priest, led the second group of captives back to Jerusalem. This pagan king recognized Yahweh as the god of the Israelites, and provided all they needed for this long journey. As a result of this royal favor, Ezra declared, "Praise (**blessed**) be Yahweh, the God of our fathers, who has put it into the king's mind to glorify the house of the LORD in Jerusalem, and who has shown favor to me before the king, and his counselors, and all his powerful officers. So I took courage because I was strengthened by Yahweh my God, and I gathered Israelite leaders to return with me." Ezra blessed the LORD because he recognized that only by God's favor was he permitted to make this journey and serve his people in this manner.

We learn from Ezra's example that it is essential to have Yahweh's hand upon us if we are to succeed in accomplishing His will. (See 8:18, 22, 31)

NEHEMIAH

This interesting servant led the third group of returnees from Babylon to Israel in about 445 B.C. His mission was to guide his fellow Israelites in rebuilding the wall around the city. In spite of strong opposition, they achieved this project in 52 days (6:15). Apart from the blessing of Yahweh, such a feat would have been impossible. Consider six references to these blessings.

8:6 Ezra the scribe read the law of Moses to the people from morning to midday, standing on a platform. When he opened the book, all the people stood with him, and he "Praised (**blessed**) the LORD, the great God. Then all the people answered. 'Amen. Amen' while lifting up their hands. And they bowed their heads and worshiped the LORD with their faces to the ground."

9:5-6 Later, the people again assembled to confess their sins, hear God's word read, and listened as the priests declared (as part of the longest prayer in the Bible), "Stand up, Praise (**bless**) the LORD your God forever and ever! Praise (**blessed**) be Your glorious name and may it be exalted above all **blessing** and praise. . . ." What a fine example for us regarding offering "blessing and praise" as central to our worship.

11:2 This reference is about the repopulating of Jerusalem. Lots were cast to see which one out of ten families would live in the city and who would remain elsewhere. "The people praised (**blessed**) all the men who volunteered to live in Jerusalem."

13:2 Part of the dedication of the new wall included another reading of Moses' law. This law stated a judgment upon outsiders who had hired Balaam to curse the Israelites. "Our God turned the curse into a **blessing**." Here's an interesting testimony to Yahweh's power to overrule threats against His people. We benefit from this same expression of His grace and mercy when evil desires are transformed into blessings.

ESTHER

The amazing events recorded in this brief book occurred during the reign of Xerxes I, ruler of Persia (486-465 B.C.), just prior to the times of Ezra and Nehemiah. Several interesting facts include the truth that the term "Jews" is found here more often than in the rest of the books of the Old Testament combined. Esther became queen around 478 B.C. as the result of a conspiracy to destroy all the Jews. In fact, this book revels more about the influence of one woman to preserve Yahweh's people than any other Bible book.

Although the terms "bless" and "blessing" are not found in the text of Esther, no other book so clearly reveals Yahweh's work, behind the scenes. Apart from His repeated and consistent blessings, these events would never have happened. And the Hebrew people would have perished. What a blessing to them and to us!

STUDY GUIDE

Prepare your responses to these questions and share them with other learners.

B Biblical Reference

Choose your favorite Scripture reference from this session and list it here. _____

Be prepared to explain your reason for this choice. _____

_____

L Learning

What new or helpful truth have you learned from this session?

_____

_____

E Example

Find an example from these biblical passages that expresses the manner in which you want to bless others. _____

_____

_____

S State

What blessing from God or from others have you received this week?

_____

_____

S Share

Tell about some way in which you recently blessed someone.

_____

_____

JOB

Some scholars believe this is the oldest book of the Bible, however, the date and author are unknown. Job, the man, is mentioned elsewhere: Ezekiel 14: 14, 20, and James 5:11. This is the first of the five Poetical or Wisdom books (others are Psalms, Proverbs, Ecclesiastes, and Song of Solomon). The book is all about one man and his friends, along with portions about God and Satan. Here is the only book dealing with the puzzling question of why would a good and sovereign God allow a righteous person to suffer? Consider five references to "bless" and blessing."

1:10 Here is the only place in the Bible where Satan speaks of Yahweh's blessing upon someone. After the LORD commends Job to Satan as being "a man of perfect integrity, who fears God and turns away from evil," Satan answered, "Does Job fear God for nothing? Have you not made a hedge around him, around his household, and around all that he has on every side? You have **blessed** the work of his hands, and his possessions have increased in the land." Satan was very aware of all the favor Yahweh had shown to His servant. And as the accuser, Satan claimed that Yahweh's favor was the reason Job was such a good person.

1:21-22 On one day Satan destroyed all of Job's possessions—his herds and flocks, and all seven of his sons. The response of Job to these great losses is found in these words of integrity: "Job arose and tore his robe and shaved his head, and he fell to the ground and worshiped. And he said: 'Naked I came from my mother's womb, and naked shall I return there. The LORD gives, and the LORD takes away. Praise **(blessed)** be the name of Yahweh.' In all this Job did not sin nor charge God with wrong." What a remarkable expression of faith and gratitude! Although he believed Yahweh had removed all these possessions from him, he maintained his sense of confidence in Yahweh's dealings with him. We can learn much from this example.

29:11-13 The intervening chapters have recounted the words of three of Job's friends who accused him of some kind of wrongdoing. They maintained the conviction that Job was being punished for his sins. Chapter 29 is the recording of Job's defense. He enumerates all his good deeds to needy persons, among which is this: "When they heard me, they **blessed** me, and when they saw me, they spoke well of me. For I rescued the poor man who cried out for help, and the fatherless child who had no one to support him. The dying man **blessed** me and I made the widow's heart rejoice." Job could not understand his suffering since he was basically a good man. Here is where we empathize with him; we often question Yahweh's dealing with us or with others who seem to suffer unjustly.

31:20 Job continues his appeal for God to remember all his good deeds; he repeats an "if" about 20 times in this chapter, all to affirm his innocence. Here is one example: "If he [a poor man] did not **bless** me while warming himself with the fleece from my sheep. . . . ." Job makes a long list of all the ways he has reached out to help the helpless, in order to justify his claim of being mistreated by God.

42:12 This chapter brings Job's story to a good conclusion—Job became aware of the purpose for his suffering and repented for his foolish complaints; his friends were rebuked by Yahweh for their bad counsel to him, and all Job's losses were more than restored. "So the LORD **blessed** the last part of Job's life more than the first. For he had fourteen thousand sheep, six thousand camels, one thousand yoke of oxen, one thousand female donkeys. He also had seven sons and three daughters." All this helps us understand that regardless of our suffering and grief, Yahweh's purpose will ultimately prevail and we will be blessed by Him. He always brings good out of life's sorrows and pain.

Consider these basic lessons for life learned from Job's experiences.

1. We should not be surprised when trouble comes; we live in a fallen world where Satan seeks to cause us to question God's love for us.

2. We should not blame God when we experience disappointments and pain. We have an enemy who works to bring grief to us.

3. We should always trust God to bring us safely through our hardships and to bless us by teaching us valuable lessons from our troubles.

PSALMS

The book of Psalms is the blessing book of the Bible with more than 100 references to the terms "bless" and "blessing." Most of these are directed god-ward—"**Bless** Yahweh, O my soul and all that is within me." But there are also many expressions of His blessing upon His people. Let's walk together to learn from many of these occurrences. (As mentioned earlier, sometimes the same Hebrew term is translated as "blessed", or "praise", or "happy.")

1:1 How fitting that the psalms begin with the word "**Blessed** is the man who walks not in the counsel of the ungodly. . . ." This opening chapter describes the blessedness of the person who delights in the law of the LORD and meditates therein day and night. Such a person is like at fruitful tree who never withers, and who prospers in all he does.

2:12 This chapter describes Yahweh's Son and declares, "**Blessed** are all those who put their trust in Him."

3:8 Here is the first among many psalms attributed to David. He celebrates Yahweh's deliverance of him from all his enemies and declares, "Salvation belongs to the LORD. Your **blessing** is upon Your people."

5:12 Again David extolls Yahweh as he concludes this psalm with, "Let all those rejoice who put their trust in You; let those also who love Your name be joyful in You. For You, O LORD, will **bless** the righteous; with favor You will surround him as with a shield."

10:3 We find here a rare reference to the act of the wicked blessing others. "For the wicked boasts of his heart's desire; he **blesses** the greedy and renounces the LORD." How inappropriate does this sound! Surely the blessing of the wicked is not something to desire.

16:7 David celebrates all Yahweh has done for Him, and he declares,"I will praise (**bless**) the LORD who has given me counsel; my heart also instructs me in the night seasons."

18:46 The psalmist offers praise to Yahweh—"The LORD lives—may my Rock be praised (**blessed**)! The God of my salvation is exalted."

21:1-3 Again David rejoices in Yahweh's favor as he says, "The king shall have joy in Your strength, O LORD, and in Your salvation how greatly shall he rejoice. You have given him his heart's desire and have not withheld the request of his lips, for you meet him with the **blessings** of goodness; You set a crown of pure gold upon his head." Notice the numerous favors David recalls. We do well to enumerate His blessings upon us. As the old song declares: "Count your many blessings, name them one by one. And it will surprise you what the Lord has done."

24:5 As David describes the person who may stand in Yahweh's holy place, he says, "He will receive **blessing** from the LORD, and righteousness from the God of his salvation."

26:12 After David asks Yahweh to examine him, he states: "As for me, I will walk in mine integrity. Redeem me and be merciful to me. My foot stands in an even place; in the congregations I will **bless** the LORD."

28:6, 9 Here is a song of praise for answered prayer: "**Blessed** be the LORD, because He has heard the voice of my supplications! The LORD is my strength and my shield, my heart trusted in Him and I am helped; therefore my heart greatly rejoices and with my song I will praise Him." He goes on to say, "Save Your people, and **bless** Your inheritance; shepherd them also, and bear them up forever."

29:11 David concludes this masterpiece of praise to Yahweh in this manner: "The LORD gives strength to His people; the LORD **blesses** His people with peace."

31:21 Various kinds of trouble surrounded David, nevertheless, he ends his lament with this beautiful tribute: "**Blessed** be the LORD, for He has shown me His marvelous kindness in a strong city!"

34:1, 8 "I will praise (**bless**) the LORD at all times; His praise shall continually be in my mouth. . . .O, taste and see that the LORD is good; how happy (**blessed**) is the man who trusts in Him!" These beautiful words express David's strong personal commitment to be continually praising Yahweh; thus blessing Him in a pleasing manner.

37:22 The final state of the righteous and the wicked are contrasted here. "Those who are **blessed** by Him shall inherit the earth, but those who are cursed by Him shall be cut off."

41:1, 2, 13 "Happy (**blessed**) is he who considers the poor; the LORD will deliver him in time of trouble. The LORD will preserve him and keep him alive, and he will be **blessed** on the earth; You will not deliver him to the will of his enemies. . . May Yahweh, the God of Israel be praised (**blessed**) from everlasting to everlasting! Amen and Amen." Here is a promise to those who reach out to help the poor: Yahweh will deliver that person in time of trouble.

45:2 This chapter is a song of love for the Messiah, as God's chosen bride. Verse 2 describes the Messiah in these lovely terms: "You are fairer than the sons of men; grace is poured upon Your lips; therefore God has **blessed** You forever."

49:18 These plaintive words describe the fate of the wicked: "Though while he lives he **blesses** himself (for men will praise you when you do well for yourself), he shall go to the generation of his father; they shall never see light. . . like the beasts that perish." What a solemn warning to those who take pride in themselves.

62:4 Again the psalmist warns the wicked of their fate: "How long will you attack a man? You shall be slain, all of you, like a leaning wall and a tottering fence. They only consult to cast him down from his high position, they delight in lies; they **bless** with their mouth but they curse inwardly."

63:4 David makes a solemn pledge to Yahweh: "Because Your lovingkindness is better than life, my lips shall praise You. Thus will I praise **(bless)** You as long as I live; I will lift up my hands in Your name. My soul shall be satisfied as with marrow and fatness, and my mouth shall praise You with joyful lips."

65:4, 9-10 Both man and nature are within God's blessing as David relates: "**Blessed** is the man You choose, and cause to approach You. . . You visit the earth and water it. . .You make it soft with showers, You **bless** its growth."

66:8, 20 This psalmist first declares his praise, the explains why such is appropriate: "Oh, **bless** our God, you peoples! And make the noise of His praise to be heard. . . **Blessed** be God, who has not turned away my prayer, nor His mercy from me!"

67:1, 6-7 These words are from a great missionary psalm: "God be merciful to us and **bless** us, and cause His face to shine upon us. That Your way may be known on earth, Your salvation among all nations. . . . God, our God, **blesses** us. God will **bless** us and all the ends of the earth will fear Him."

68:19, 26, 35 David's song of praise enumerates many of Yahweh's blessings, then responds with: "**Blessed** be the LORD, who daily loads us with benefits. The God of our salvation. . . **Bless** God in the congregations, the LORD, from the fountain of Israel. . . **Blessed** be God."

72:17-19 Solomon may have authored these noble words about Yahweh: "His name shall endure forever; His name shall continue as long as the sun. And men shall be **blessed** in Him; all nations shall call Him **blessed**. **Blessed** be the LORD God, the God of Israel, who only does wondrous things! And **blessed** be His glorious name forever!

50

84:4-5, 12 Three "blesseds" are recorded in this psalm celebrating the presence of Yahweh in His "house." First, "**Blessed** are those who dwell in Your house; they will still be praising You." And "**Blessed** is the man whose strength is in You." Finally, "**Blessed** is the man who trusts in You." Here is another way of declaring how very fortunate is the person who knows Yahweh and trusts in Him.

(Some translations use "happy" in place of "blessed" here and elsewhere.)

89:15, 52 This lovely song is attributed to Ethan, the Ezrahite, who celebrates the faithfulness of Yahweh to His covenant with David. He declares, "**Blessed** are the people who know the joyful sound," and concludes with "**Blessed** be the LORD forevermore." From the context we conclude that the "joyful sound" is just the sound of the name "Yahweh," what joy His name and His nature bring!

94:12 This unknown writer worships the LORD for teaching him, by saying: "**Blessed** is the man whom You instruct, O LORD, and teach out of Your law."

96:1-2 "Oh, sing unto the LORD a new song! Sing to the LORD, all the earth. Sing to the Yahweh, **bless** His name; proclaim the good news of His salvation from day to day." Here is a good reminder that our worship songs must be directed to Yahweh and should focus on His name (Yahweh) and all the marvelous works He does.

100:4 A brief call to worship is found in these very meaningful words which tell us how to approach Yahweh: "Enter into His gates with thanksgiving, and into His courts with praise. Be thankful to Him and **bless** His name."

103:1-2, 20-22 This song of praise has more references to "bless" than any other psalm, in fact, it begins and ends with "bless." Notice the three strong commands at the beginning to "bless the LORD." First, "**Bless** the LORD, O my soul; and all that is within me." Next, "**bless** His holy name." Then, "**Bless** the LORD, O my soul, and forget not all His benefits"—followed by a statement of five of these personal benefits.

The psalm closes with a call to four entities to bless Him: "**Bless** the LORD, you His angels. . . **Bless** the LORD, all you His hosts. . . **Bless** the LORD, all His works. . . **Bless** the LORD, O my soul." What a glorious combination of all the LORD's creation to join in exalting Him with their praise!

(Again, some translations render "bless" as "praise" here and elsewhere.)

104:1, 35 Here Yahweh is praised for all His amazing works of creation. "**Bless** the LORD" comes first and last, like a parenthesis. He is worthy of all blessing and praise for all His wondrous creation!

106:3, 48 This historian recounts the merciful and mighty acts of Yahweh on behalf of His chosen people beginning with their bondage in Egypt, followed by their experiences under the leadership of Moses and later, Joshua. Then their rebellion and captivity are mentioned, but finally Yahweh remembered His covenant and delivered them. Then come these very appropriate words of praise: "**Blessed** be Yahweh, the God of Israel from everlasting to everlasting! And let all the people say, 'Amen!' Praise the LORD!"

107:38 What wonderful and merciful acts of Yahweh are enumerated here. And in the midst of these we find the psalmist saying, "He also **blesses** them." Truth is—all these amazing works of His are expressions of His blessings.

109:17, 28 David describes the words and deeds of the wicked against him. He asks the LORD to withhold His blessing from these enemies. He closes his list of the actions of the wicked by saying, "Let them curse, but You **bless**; when they arise let them be ashamed, but let Your servant rejoice."

112:1-2 The psalmist begins this chapter with a strong statement of God's blessing upon the righteous man and his descendants: "**Blessed** is the man who fears the LORD, who delights greatly in His commandments. His descendants will be mighty on earth; the generation of the upright will be **blessed**."

113:2 Here is a statement regarding the duration and extension of blessing the name of the LORD: "**Blessed** be Yahweh, the name of the LORD! From this time forth and forevermore! From the rising of the sun to its going down the LORD's name is to be praised." In other words, we should bless the LORD always and everywhere!

115:12-13, 15, 18 First, we are told who Yahweh has blessed and will bless: "The LORD has been mindful of us; He will **bless** us; He will **bless** the house of Israel; He will **bless** the house of Aaron; He will **bless** those who fear the LORD, both small and great." Then a short **benediction**: "May the LORD give you increase more and more, you and your children. May you be **blessed** by the LORD who made heaven and earth." And finally, "But we will **bless** the LORD from this time forth and forevermore."

118:26 The LORD's name "Yahweh" occurs 28 times in this messianic psalm. Two of these references are found in verse 26: "**Blessed** is he who comes in the name of the LORD! We have **blessed** you from the house of the LORD."

119:1-2, 12 This acrostic poem with 22 sections, corresponding to the letters of the Hebrew alphabet, has three strong references to "blessed." First, "**Blessed** are the undefiled in the way, who walk in the law of the LORD! **Blessed** are those who keep His testimonies, who seek Him with the whole heart!" And "**Blessed** are You, O LORD! Teach me Your statutes." Here is the longest chapter in the Bible, coming next to the Bible's middle chapter, Psalm 118. Thus in the very heart of God's Word we have these promises of blessedness upon those who revere His written truth!

124:6 The LORD's defense of His people is celebrated in this poem. "**Blessed** be the LORD, who has not given us as prey to their teeth. Our soul has escaped as a bird from the snare of the fowlers; the snare is broken and we have escaped."

128:1, 4, 5 Here is a clear reference to the blessedness of those who fear the LORD. "**Blessed** is everyone who fears the LORD, who walks in His ways. . . Behold, thus shall the man be **blessed** who fears the LORD. . .

The LORD **bless** you out of Zion, and may you see the good of Jerusalem all the days of your life."

129:8 Here us a rather unusual reference to a spoken blessing. The psalmist is celebrating the victory of Yahweh's people over their enemies; he says of these foes, "Neither let those who pass by them say, 'The **blessing** of the LORD be upon you; we **bless** you in the name of the LORD.'" In other words, Do not speak words of blessing upon those who hate Zion!

132:15 The psalmist declares that Yahweh has chosen Zion as His place of habitation, His resting place forever. Therefore, He says, "I will abundantly **bless** her provision; I will satisfy her poor with bread. I will also clothe her priests with salvation, and her saints shall shout aloud for joy."

133:3 The blessed unity of Yahweh's people is the theme of this song of ascents. As the people walked up to the temple mount, they sang, "It is like the dew of Hermon, descending upon the mountains of Zion; for there the LORD commanded the **blessing**—life forevermore." How interesting to hear the truth that Yahweh's ultimate blessing upon His people is eternal life—with Him!

134:1-3 A brief psalm with three "blessings." "Behold, **bless** the LORD, all you servants of the LORD, who by night stand in the house of the LORD! Lift up your hands in the sanctuary, and **bless** the LORD. The LORD who made heaven and earth **bless** you from Zion!"

135:19-21 Here is another strong emphasis on His people blessing the LORD. "**Bless** the LORD, O house of Israel! **Bless** the LORD, O house of Aaron! **Bless** the LORD, O house of Levi! You who fear the LORD, bless the LORD! **Blessed** be the LORD out of Zion, who dwells in Jerusalem."

144:1-2 David praises Yahweh for His preservation and prosperity: "**Blessed** be the LORD my Rock, who trains my hands for war, and my fingers for battle—my lovingkindness and my fortress, my high tower and my deliverer, my shield, and the One in whom I take refuge, who subdues my people under me." How interesting that in the midst of this warfare context, David calls Yahweh, "my lovingkindness."

145:1-2, 10, 21 Another song of David gives strong emphasis to the importance of giving praise to Yahweh: "I will extol you, my God, O King, and I will **bless** your name forever and ever. Every day I will **bless** you, and I will praise Your name forever and ever. . . All Your works shall praise You, O LORD, and Your saints shall **bless** You. . . My mouth shall speak the praise of the LORD, and all flesh shall **bless** His holy name forever and ever." Notice the clear emphasis on praise and blessing belonging together.

147:13 In the midst of this song of praise comes these words: "He strengthens the bars of your gates and **blesses** your children within you." Ending these many references to "bless" in the psalms, comes this final declaration: "Yahweh blesses your children." What an amazing compilation of some 107 references to "bless" and "blessing" in this single volume!

(Psalms is the middle book of the Bible, so we are approximately half-way through this study.)

STUDY GUIDE

Prepare your responses to these questions and share them with other learners.

B Biblical Reference

Choose your favorite Scripture reference from this session and list it here. _____

Be prepared to explain your reason for this choice. _____

_____

L Learning

What new or helpful truth have you learned from this session?

_____

_____

E Example

Find an example from these biblical passages that expresses the manner in which you want to bless others. _____

_____

_____

S State

What blessing from God or from others have you received this week?

_____

_____

S Share

Tell about some way in which you recently blessed someone.

_____

_____

PROVERBS

Known as the wisdom book of the Bible, this most interesting and helpful volume is noted for its practical advice. Most of these brief and succinct statements come from the pen of Solomon, son of David and Bathsheba. Consider these words from 1 Kings 4:29 -34: "God gave Solomon wisdom and exceedingly great understanding, and largeness of heart like the sand on the seashore. Thus Solomon's wisdom excelled the wisdom of all the men of the East and all the wisdom of Egypt. For he was wiser than all men . . . and his fame was in all the surrounding nations. He spoke three thousand proverbs, and his songs were one thousand and five . . . and men of all nations, from all the king of the earth who had heard of his wisdom came to hear the wisdom of Solomon."

Some portions of this book were written by Agur and Lemuel, but most by Solomon. (He also wrote Ecclesiastes and Song of Solomon.) The date of writing these 900 proverbs would be about 950-700 B.C. What Psalms are to our devotional life, Proverbs are to our practical life. "Psalms for my worship; Proverbs for my walk." Proverbs are described as short sayings based on long experience; they are short, concise statements conveying moral truths. Whereas knowledge is a matter of having facts, wisdom is the application of facts to life. "You can get knowledge from college, but wisdom comes from God."

A key statement is found in 9:10 "The fear of the LORD is the beginning of wisdom, and knowledge of the Holy One is understanding."

Our study of the terms "bless" and "blessed" will include sixteen references in the book of Proverbs.

3:33 "The curse of the LORD is on the house of the wicked, but He **blesses** the habitation of the just." Here is a contrast of what the wicked and the just can expect from Yahweh.

5:18 "Let your fountain be **blessed**, and rejoice with the wife of your youth." These words come from the context of marriage. Solomon advised men to find sexual satisfaction from their own wives and not from someone outside their marriage. Unfortunately he did not follow his own counsel later in life.

8:32, 34 These words are from a personification of wisdom: "Now therefore, listen to me, my children, for **blessed** are those who keep my ways. Hear instruction and be wise, and do not disdain it. **Blessed** is the man who listens to me, watching daily at my gates, waiting at the posts of my doors." Note the emphasis on "listen" and "hear instruction." The wise person pays close attention to the counsel of a wise teacher.

10:6, 7, 22 "**Blessings** are on the head of the righteous, but violence covers the mouth of the wicked. The memory of the righteous is **blessed**, but the name of the wicked will rot." Again we see the contrast between the righteous and the wicked. Then, "The **blessing** of the LORD makes one rich and He adds no sorrow with it." True riches, that which cannot be lost or stolen, comes from the LORD's blessing, not from temporal material wealth.

11:11 "By the **blessing** of the upright the city is exalted, but it is overthrown by the mouth of the wicked." Those citizens who are righteous are a true blessing to fellow inhabitants, while the words of wicked persons bring downfall. The wholesome influence of godly persons lift an entire city, but evil talkers bring its destruction.

11:26 "The people will curse him who withholds grain, but **blessing** will be on the head of him who sells it." Here is a picture of people who are starving for want of food, but those who have food and keep it for themselves are cursed for their lack of compassion. On the other hand, those who share their food with the needy are blessed by them and by the LORD.

20:7 "The righteous man walks in his integrity; his children are **blessed** after him." A parent whose lifestyle is described as one of integrity (wholeness) will prove to be a blessing to his children. Godliness produces a wholesome influence on succeeding generations.

20:21 "An inheritance gained hastily at the beginning will not be **blessed** at the end." The person who seeks to gain wealth before it is due to him will not find Yahweh's favor later.

22:9 "He who has a bountiful eye will be **blessed**, for he gives of his bread to the poor." A "bountiful eye" refers to the person who looks upon the needy and seeing their condition reaches out to help them; such a person will be blessed by the LORD.

24:25 "But those who rebuke the wicked will have delight, and a good **blessing** will come upon them." The context here concerns the proper treatment of evil persons—to call them righteous brings disfavor from others, while condemnation results in favor from them.

28:20 "A faithful man will abound with **blessings**, but he who hastens to be rich will not go unpunished." A person whose values are spiritual and thus seeks to be faithful to God and in his dealings with people will have an abundance of true blessings. But the person whose primary object in life is to accumulate wealth will ultimately suffer for it.

30:11 "There is a generation that curses its father, and does not **bless** its mother." Solomon uses four verses to describe an evil generation of people who, among other sins, disrespect their parents. He states this as a warning to readers.

31:28 "Her children rise up and call her **blessed**; her husband also, and he praises her." Chapter 31 has more to say about a virtuous wife than any other portion of scripture. The chapter is attributed to "King Lemuel" (v. 1) which may refer to Solomon, If so, these words describe his mother, Bathsheba. One result of her diligent care for her family is their appreciation and praise for her. From verse 10 to the end of the chapter, this passage is an acrostic poem based on the 22 letters of the Hebrew alphabet. Each verse begins with the succeeding letter of the alphabet. This was a favorite form of composition and aided in the memory of what was written. Verse 28 begins with the Hebrew letter Koph. Verse 30 states the secret of such a virtuous person: "Charm is deceitful and beauty is vain, but a woman who fears the LORD, she shall be praised."

As we discovered in 9:10, "the fear of Yahweh is the beginning of wisdom." That person, like the virtuous wife, who desires to behave wisely in all human and divine relationships will give highest value to giving due respect and honor to Yahweh, the LORD of hosts.

ECCLESIASTES

The writer of this interesting book identifies himself in verse 1 as "the Preacher, the son of David, king in Jerusalem." Most interpreters believe this was Solomon who also wrote Proverbs and the Song of Solomon. Contents of this work indicate these words were probably composed later in Solomon's life, as he looked back on years of personal experience.

Greek translators gave the title "Ecclesiastes" meaning "one who assembles people," akin to *ecclesia*, "an assembly." The original Hebrew title was *Ooheleth,* meaning "preacher" or "teacher." Thus many references are made to the Preacher, such as in 1:1 "Vanity of vanities, says the Preacher, all is vanity" (repeated at the close 12:8). This term "vanity" occurs more than 30 times in this book, but only once elsewhere in the Bible.

Vanity, as used here, refers to something without significance or meaning. Here is the humanistic view of life; life apart from Yahweh. A summary of the teaching of Ecclesiastes is that "although human beings can accumulate many things, accomplish much, and achieve great wisdom, these are without profit and ultimately pointless, unless one has lived in the fear of and obedience to God."

Solomon brings his sometimes random thoughts to a clear conclusion: "Let us hear the conclusion of the whole matter: Fear God and keep His commandments, for this is the whole duty of man. For God will bring every work into judgment, including every secret thing, whether it is good or whether it is evil" (12:13-14).

Another interesting feature of this book is the fact that there is but one reference to our word "blessed." Perhaps this is a testimony to the fact that those who choose to live a humanistic way of life miss the blessed life of a believer.

10:16-17 "Woe to you, O land, when your king is a child, and your princes feast in the morning! **Blessed** are you, O land, when your king is the son of nobles, and your princes feast at the proper time—for strength and not for drunkenness." Here is a rather strange contrast between two kinds of rulers, one brings woe, the other a blessing. We have examples of this in nations today.

SONG OF SOLOMON

The Hebrew title is *Shir Hashirim* meaning "The Best Song," and sometimes referred to as *Canticles*, the Latin term for "songs." Probably written by Solomon (as verse one declares) when he was a young man. We are told (1 Kings 4:32) that he wrote 1,005 songs; this may be one of them, if so, this is the only one preserved for our reading.

We have a fine example of Hebrew poetry describing the beauty of intimate love between a man and his wife (perhaps a bride and groom). At times erotic, none-the-less candid regarding the passionate affection between two lovers.

Some interpreters see this as an allegory depicting the love between Christ and His bride—the church. We know that the apostle Paul used that metaphor several times in his writing.

As in Ecclesiastes, there is a single reference to "blessed."

6:8-9 When "The Beloved" (Solomon) speaks lovingly of his bride "The Shulamite," he says, "There are sixty queens and eighty concubines, and virgins without number. My dove, my perfect one, is the only one, the only one of her mother, the favorite of the one who bore her. The daughters saw her and called her **blessed**, the queens and the concubines and they praised her."

If we follow the allegorical line of interpretation, we can easily see how the Bride of Christ is worthy of being called blessed. Surely God has set her apart to be blessed and to be His blessing to all persons who believe.

ISAIAH

Now we begin the final section of the Old Testament--17 books of the prophets. These are traditionally divided as five major and 12 minor prophetic books; based on the length of these writings.

The first and perhaps most significant work is that of Isaiah, whose name means "Yahweh saves." He lived in the southern kingdom of Judah where he served the LORD from about 740 B.C. until 701 B.C. Isaiah was married and had two sons.

His message from God was that because of Judah's continued idolatry they would be sent into Babylonian captivity. However, due to His mercy and grace, Yahweh would provide a Savior who would take away their sins and restore them to their homeland, so that His kingdom would be unending in the new heavens and new earth.

We will consider twelve references to the terms "bless" and "blessed."

19:24, 25 "In that day Israel will be one of three with Egypt and Assyria, even a **blessing** in the midst of the land, whom the LORD of hosts shall **bless** saying, '**Blessed** is Egypt My people, and Assyria the work of My hands, and Israel My inheritance.'" The prophet is speaking of a future "day" when Israel, along with two of their chief enemies—Egypt and Assyria will turn to Yahweh and all will become God's blessing among the nations. What a miraculous change that will be! Only God can do such wondrous things; truly His blessings.

30:18 "Therefore the LORD will wait, that He may be gracious to you; and therefore He will be exalted, that He may have mercy on you. For the LORD is a God of justice; **blessed** are all those who wait for Him."

Here are words that give hope to God's wayward people. Notice the terms "gracious" and "mercy." All who "wait," that is, put their trust in Him will experience His blessing.

32:20 "**Blessed** are you who sow beside all waters, who send out freely the feet of the ox and the donkey." These words come at the conclusion of a passage where the LORD describes the prosperity that will come to His people when His Spirit is poured out upon them—their crops and their cattle will enjoy abundance.

44:3 "For I will pour water on him who is thirsty, and floods on the dry ground; I will pour My Spirit on your descendants, and My **blessing** on your offspring." These words were fulfilled on the Day of Pentecost when God poured out His Spirit upon His church. No other blessing compares to this for its benefits.

51:2-3 "Look to Abraham your father, and to Sarah who bore you; for I called him alone, and **blessed** him and increased him. For the LORD will comfort Zion, He will comfort all her waste places; He will make her wilderness like Eden, and her desert like the garden of the LORD; joy and gladness will be found in it, thanksgiving and the voice of melody." Yahweh speaks here of His blessing upon Abraham, and His promise to bless His people in the future. How comforting were these words to Isaiah's hearers.

56:1-2 "Thus says the LORD; 'Keep justice and do righteousness, for My salvation is about to come, and My righteousness to be revealed. **Blessed** is the man who does this and the son of man who lays hold on it; who keeps from defiling the Sabbath, and keeps his hand from doing any evil." This chapter states God's promises to include the Gentiles in His plans for future blessings. All people of all nations are a part of God's plan of salvation and blessing.

61:8-9 "For I, the LORD, love justice; I hate robbery for burnt offering, I will direct their work in truth, and will make with them an everlasting covenant. Their descendants shall be known among the Gentiles, and their offspring among the people. All who see them shall acknowledge them, that they are the posterity whom the LORD has **blessed**." God promises to bless all people and make His covenant inclusive of all who put their trust in Him.

65:8 "As the new wine is found in the cluster, and one says, 'Do not destroy it, for a **blessing** is in it.' So will I do for my servants' sake, that I may not destroy them all." Here is Yahweh's promise of mercy to those who have forsaken Him.

65:23 "They shall not labor in vain, nor bring forth children for trouble; for they shall be the descendants of the **blessed** of the LORD, and their offspring with them." The context for these words are a description of the future "new heavens and new earth." Note the phrase: "descendants of the **blessed** of the LORD." We are the blessed of the LORD, and our children, their children, and so on will inherit this blissful existence.

66:3 "He who kills a bull as if he slays a man; he who sacrifices a lamb, as if he breaks a dog's neck; he who offers a grain offering, as if he offers swine's blood; he who burns incense as if he **blessed** an idol. Just as they have chosen their own ways and their soul delights in their abominations," Here is a final warning to those worshipers whose offerings are insincere and pretentious. None will be accepted, and Yahweh will bring His judgment on all such hypocrisy.

JEREMIAH

Yahweh called Jeremiah to be a prophet when he was a young man and used him mightily for 40 years. He served under the final five kings of the southern kingdom of Judah. His ministry occurred about 60 years after Isaiah. More is known about Jeremiah than of any other prophet; his writings are very autobiographical. His message was one of condemning the leaders of Judah for their idolatry, warning them of God's impending judgment. However, he also offered hope for their future—after 70 years of captivity in Babylon.

Consider the two references to "bless":

4:1-2 "'If you will return, O Israel,' says the LORD, 'Return to Me; and if you will put away your abominations out of My sight, then you shall not be moved. And you shall swear, 'The LORD lives,' in truth, in judgment, and in righteousness; the nations shall **bless** themselves in Him, and in Him shall they glory.'" A continuing theme in Jeremiah's messages is that of a call to repentance—to forsake their idols in order to worship only Him. Here He promises stability to them as well as a clear testimony to other nations. As a result of this, other nations will bring favor to themselves and go on to give praise to Him.

31:23 "Thus says the LORD of hosts, the God of Israel: 'They shall again use this speech in the land of Judah and in its cities when I bring back their captivity: "The LORD **bless** you O habitation of justice, and mountain of holiness!"'" Here is the promise of future blessings upon Judah—a benediction that will be commonly declared when they return from captivity in Babylon.

This chapter also contains Jeremiah's version of Yahweh's new covenant with His people—truly the blessing of all blessings!

31:31-34 "'Behold the days are coming,' says the LORD, 'when I will make a new covenant with the house of Israel and with the house of Judah—not according to the covenant I made with their fathers in the day that I took them by the hand to bring them out of the land of Egypt, My covenant which they broke, though I was a husband to them,' says the LORD. 'But this is the covenant that I will make with the house of Israel: after those days,' says the LORD, 'I will put My law in their minds, and write it on their hearts; and I will be their God, and they shall be My people. No more shall every man teach his neighbor, and every man his brother, saying, "Know the LORD," for they shall all know Me, from the least of them to the greatest of them," says the LORD, 'For I will forgive their iniquity, and their sin I will remember no more.'" (We will find similar references to this new covenant in Ezekiel 11:19-20 and 36:26-29.)

LAMENTATIONS

This unique book of the Bible expresses the grief felt by the author over the destruction of Jerusalem and the Temple on August 14, 586 B.C. The Babylonian army, under the command of Nebuchadnezzar came against the holy city three times before it finally fell. Most interpreters consider Jerimiah, the "Weeping Prophet" to be the writer of this lament. He had repeatedly given the people and her leaders God's warning of impending disaster due to their rebellion against Him. And he lived to see these warnings fulfilled.

However, in the midst of the prophet's expressions of grief, one bright hope shone forth in the most often quoted portion of this brief book: "Through the LORD's mercies we are not consumed. Because His compassions fail not. They are new every morning; great is Your faithfulness. 'The LORD is my portion,' says my soul, 'therefore I hope in Him'" (3:22-24).

Although there are no occurrences of the terms "bless" and "blessed," in Lamentations, this passage alone speaks volumes regarding Yahweh's favor upon His people in spite of their total unworthiness.

STUDY GUIDE

Prepare your responses to these questions and share them with other learners.

B Biblical Reference

Choose your favorite Scripture reference from this session and list it here. _____

Be prepared to explain your reason for this choice. _____

_____

L Learning

What new or helpful truth have you learned from this session?

_____

_____

E Example

Find an example from these biblical passages that expresses the manner in which you want to bless others. _____

_____

_____

S State

What blessing from God or from others have you received this week?

_____

_____

S Share

Tell about some way in which you recently blessed someone.

_____

_____

EZEKIEL

His name means "God will strengthen." He was a contemporary with Jeremiah and Daniel, and was about 25 years old when he was taken to Babylon as a captive in 597 B.C. Ezekiel served Yahweh as a priest and a prophet among the Jewish exiles in Babylon for about 22 years, until 575 B.C. His home was beside the Chebar River, about 50 miles from the capital city of Babylon.

He was a prophet of visions. The key text of his book reads: "As I was among the captives . . . the heavens were opened, and I saw visions of God." Many of his visions compare to those of John in the Revelation, in fact these two books must be read together in order to understand the meaning of similar visions. Ezekiel and Daniel are the apocalypses (revelations) of the Old Testament.

The term "glory of God" is one of the themes of his writings, appearing 12 times in the first 11 chapters. Ezekiel's message to the Jews was a warning—they lost their homeland due to their sins—the glory of the LORD departed from them and their city and its temple were destroyed. He called upon his people to repent and return to Yahweh. His book ends with the promise of future glory for his people.

Consider four references to "bless" and "blessing" in Ezekiel's writings.

3:12 "Then the Spirit lifted me up, and I heard behind me a great thunderous voice: '**Blessed** is the glory of the LORD from His place.'" Here is Ezekiel's testimony regarding God's commission to go as a watchman to his own people: "Son of man, I have made you a watchman for the house of Israel; therefore hear a word from My mouth, and give them warning from Me . . . I will open your mouth, and you shall say to them ; Thus says the Lord God.' He who hears, let him hear; and he who refuses let him refuse; for they are a rebellious house." (3:17, 27).

34:26, 30 "I will make them and the places all around My hill a **blessing**; and I will cause showers to come down in their season; there shall be showers of **blessing** . . . Thus they shall know that I, Yahweh, their God, am with them, and that they, the house of Israel, are My people, says the Lord God.'" Thus Ezekiel not only gave warnings to the people, calling upon them to repent and return to their true and living God; he also spoke words of restoration and hope. Some of his predictions regarding the future include the final coming of the Messiah and His kingdom.

From this text come the words to an old hymn written by an evangelist, Daniel Whittle (1840-1901). He began reading the New Testament, given to him by his mother, when he became a prisoner during the Civil War. Later, he became a successful business man, then a preacher.

> There shall be showers of blessing, this is the promise of love;
> There shall be showers refreshing, sent from the Savior above.
> Showers of blessing, showers of blessing we need: mercy drops
> round us are falling, but for the showers we plead.

44:30 "The best of all first fruits of any kind, and every sacrifice of any kind from all your sacrifices, shall be the priest's; also you shall give to the priest the first of your ground meal, to cause a **blessing** to rest on your house." These final chapters refer to the restoration of the Jews to their homeland in Israel; first after 70 years of Babylonian captivity, but also a final complete restoration of all God's people.

Before leaving this material let's review Ezekiel's words regarding the greatest of all God's blessings—the New Covenant.

11:19-20 "I will give them one heart, and I will put a new spirit within them, and take the stony heart out of their flesh that they may walk in My statutes and keep my judgments and do them; and they shall be my people, and I will be their God."

36:26-27 "I will give you a new heart and put a new spirit within you; I will take the heart of stone out of your flesh and give you a heart of flesh. I will put My spirit within you and cause you to walk in My statues and you will keep My judgments and do them."

These words refer to the New Covenant mentioned by Jesus at the Last Supper; a covenant fulfilled on the Day of Pentecost when the Holy Spirit came upon all believers and worked the miracle of a new birth. Ever since then, we who believe have a new nature, that of the Holy Spirit living within us.

DANIEL

His name means "God Judges" and his writings as well as his personal experiences reveal the active judgment of God upon both Jews and Gentiles. Daniel was one of the choice young Jews in Jerusalem who were taken captive to Babylon in 605 BC. He was in the palace in Babylon while Ezekiel was among the slaves by the River Chebar, about 50 miles north of Babylon.

Daniel has often been called "The Prophet of Dreams," due to his God-given ability to interpret the dreams of Nebuchadnezzar, ruler of Babylon. Daniel's writings are quoted most often in the Revelation and are apocalyptic in nature. He served Yahweh in Babylon from the age of 16 until he was over 90, working under four rulers there: Nebuchadnezzar, Belshazzar, Darius, and Cyrus. Unlike the other OT prophets, Daniel's words apply most often to Gentile nations rather than the Jews.

Consider five references regarding the term "blessed."

2:19-20 "Then the secret was revealed to Daniel in a night vision. So Daniel **blessed** the God of heaven . . . and said, '**Blessed** be the name of God forever and ever, for wisdom and might are His.'" Here is the first instance when Yahweh made known to Daniel the meaning of the king's dream.

3:28 "Nebuchadnezzar spoke, saying, '**Blessed** be the God of Shadrach, Meshach, and Abed-Nego, who sent His Angel and delivered His servants who trusted in Him, and they have frustrated the king's word, and yielded their bodies that they should not serve nor worship any god except their own God!'" Here is the fiery furnace experience where Yahweh protected His three servants who trusted Him for deliverance.

4:34 "And at the end of the time I, Nebuchadnezzar, lifted my eyes to heaven, and my understanding returned to me; and I **blessed** the Most High and praised and honored Him who lives forever; for His dominion is an everlasting dominion, and His kingdom is from generation to generation." This pagan ruler behaved like an insane man until God awakened him to this realization. Here was another dream which Daniel accurately interpreted.

12:12 "**Blessed** be he who waits, and comes to the one thousand three hundred and thirty-five days. But you, go your way till the end; for you shall rest, and will arise to your inheritance at the end of the days." The final verse of Daniel's book is part of a prophecy which looks to the distant future, beginning with the 1,000 year reign of Christ.

Minor Prophets

The final division of the Old Testament covers 12 Minor Prophets; these are called Minor Prophets due to the fact that their writings are much shorter than the five previous Major Prophet books. These significant books cover the years from about 848 BC until the close of the Old Testament in 400 BC. During this time the nation of Israel was divided into the Northern (10 tribes), known as "Israel" and the Southern (2 tribes), known as "Judah." The northern tribes were overcome by the Assyrians and taken into captivity around 722 BC, while the southern tribes remained until captured by the Babylonians in 586 BC. All the Minor Prophets served as God's messengers to His people throughout this period, warning them of His impending judgment due to their unfaithfulness to Him.

Only four of these twelve books contain references to "bless" or "blessing." We will examine each of these seven occurrences.

JOEL

The date of this prophecy is uncertain, but may be among the earliest of the Minor Prophets. If so, he was sent by Yahweh to warn Judah of His judgment upon them unless they repented:

2:12-14 "'Now therefore, 'says the LORD. 'Turn to Me with all your heart, with fasting, with weeping, and with mourning. So rend your heart, and not your garments; return to the LORD your God, for He is gracious and merciful, slow to anger, and of great kindness; and He relents from doing harm. Who knows if He will turn and relent, and leave a **blessing** behind Him—a grain offering and a drink offering for the LORD your God.'"

Notice the promise of Yahweh's blessing if they chose to turn to Him with sincere and genuine repentance. One further promise of this blessing is found in these words which are quoted by Peter in the New Testament as being fulfilled on the Day of Pentecost: "And it shall come to pass afterward that I will pour out My Spirit on all flesh; your sons and your daughters shall prophesy, and your old men shall dream dreams, your young men shall see visions; and also on My menservants and on My maidservants I will pour out My Spirit in those days" (2:28-29).

Here is another widely quoted statement from this prophet: "Multitudes, multitudes in the valley of decision! For the day of the LORD is near in the valley of decision." The phrase "day of the LORD" occurs five times in Joel, more than in any other book of the Bible, and generally refers to the time when Christ shall return. However, for us there is a sense in which every day is the day of the LORD.

HAGGAI

Most of the OT prophets ministered before the fall of Israel in 722 BC, then Ezekiel and Daniel served Yahweh during the exile. Finally, three of these Minor Prophets: Haggai, Zechariah, and Malachi, are post-exilic, serving Yahweh following the return of His people from their 70-year exile in Babylon.

The first verse in Haggai confirms his date as 520 BC. His book is a series of four dated messages which Yahweh gave him to declare, urging His people to rise up and rebuild their temple in Jerusalem. His was the first prophetic voice to be heard after the first exiles returned to their homeland. When the people first came back, they laid the foundation for the temple, but then became involved with building their own houses. So for about 15 years the work on the temple was neglected. This is when Haggai was sent to stir up the people, and four years later the temple was completed. He and Zechariah were contemporaries.

2:18-19 "Consider now from this day forward, from the twenty-fourth day of the ninth month, from this day that the foundation of the LORD's temple was laid—consider it; is the seed still in the barn? As yet the vine, the fig tree, the pomegranate, and the olive tree have not yielded fruit. But from this day forward I will **bless** you." These words of Yahweh are from Haggai's third message, assuring the people that if they will pursue the task of rebuilding the temple, He will bless them. Sure enough their task was completed in four years. More than five hundred years later, Jesus taught at this same structure.

ZECHARIAH

This young prophet was born in Babylon and accompanied the exiles who returned to Jerusalem. He was a contemporary with the older prophet Haggai. Due to the length of his work, he is sometimes referred to as the "Major Minor Prophet." Furthermore, because of the numerous references to future events, his prophecy is considered to be the apocalypse of the Old Testament, much as the book of Revelation in the New Testament. His words give detailed descriptions of the experiences of Jesus, more than any other OT book. Also, of the Minor Prophets, Zechariah's message deals more with his visions (8) than any of the others.

His messages were basically words of encouragement to the returned exiles, assuring them of a better future. He emphasized Yahweh's mercy, not due to His people's merit, but for His own name's sake. This is clearly seen in these quotes.

8:13 "And it shall come to pass that just as you were a curse among the nations, O house of Judah and house of Israel, so I will save you, and you shall be a **blessing.** Do not fear, let your hands be strong."

11:4-5 "'Thus says the LORD my God, 'feed the flock for slaughter, whose owners slaughter them and feel no guilt; those who sell them say, "**Blessed** be the LORD, for I am rich"'; 'and their shepherds do not pity them.'"

MALACHI

These final three OT books give strong emphasis to God's name as "the LORD of hosts." (Occurring more than 90 times.) The Hebrew translation is *Yahweh Sabaoth*, referring to God's sovereignty over all creation—all the planets, stars, angels (both holy and fallen), all humankind, and all the events of history, as we know them. Malachi uses this term a total of 24 times. Such as:

"For from the rising of the sun, even to its going down, My name shall be great among the Gentiles. In every place incense shall be offered to My name, and a pure offering; for My name shall be great among the nations, says the LORD of hosts" (1:11).

Malachi's name means "My messenger," and that was his primary role as a prophet. His book opens with, "'I have loved you,' says Yahweh." He goes on to give many examples of God's love for them—in spite of their unworthiness. Malachi's approach to giving Yahweh's word is unique in that he asks and answers 23 questions.

Most of Malachi's warnings are to the priests and other leaders, such as this quote:

2:1-2 "'And now, O priests, this commandment is for you. If you will not hear, and if you will not take it to heart, to give glory to My name,' says the LORD of hosts, 'I will send a curse upon you, and I will curse your **blessings**. Yes, I have cursed them already, because you do not take it to heart.'" One of the functions of the priests was to pronounce God's blessings upon the people. Here Yahweh warns that unless these leaders heed His command to give glory to His name, their spoken blessings would become more of a curse.

Malachi also gave the clearest Old Testament prophesy concerning the role of John the Baptist in these words: "Behold I send My messenger, and He will prepare the way before Me. And the Lord, whom you seek will suddenly come to His temple, even the Messenger of the covenant, in whom you delight. Behold, He is coming,' says the LORD of hosts'" (3:1). It was over 400 years before this promise was fulfilled in the persons of John the Baptist and Jesus.

Another well-known statement from this prophet is found in these words: "For I am Yahweh, I do not change; therefore you are not consumed, O sons of Jacob (like Jacob, his descendants were guilty of changing frequently)." It is this changelessness of Yahweh that assures His people of hope in all circumstances of life. What a blessing we find in this immutability of our Lord.

And now we come to the final OT occurrence of the word blessing, which is the strongest promise Yahweh makes regarding His desire to bless.

3:10-12 "Bring all the tithes into the storehouse, that there may be food in My house, and prove Me now in this,' says the LORD of hosts, 'If I will not pour out for you such **blessing**, that there will not be room enough to receive it . . . And all nations will call you **blessed** for you will be a delightful land,' says the LORD of hosts."

75

Just prior to these words, Yahweh asked this probing question of His people, "Will a man rob God?" His answer, "Yet you have robbed Me!" But you say, "In what ways have we robbed You"? "In tithes and offerings. You are cursed with a curse, for you have robbed Me. Even this whole nation." Then follows Yahweh's command followed by His challenge to prove Him (put Him to a test). Only here in the entire Bible do we find such a bold invitation from God. Simply put, if we will be faithful in bringing God's tithes along with our offerings to His house of worship, He promises to literally "pour out for you such a **blessing** that there will not be room enough to receive it"!

What a beautiful way to conclude this Old Testament study of Yahweh's blessings and benedictions.

STUDY GUIDE

Prepare your responses to these questions and share them with other learners.

B Biblical Reference

Choose your favorite Scripture reference from this session and list it here. _____

Be prepared to explain your reason for this choice. _____

_____

L Learning

What new or helpful truth have you learned from this session?

_____

_____

E Example

Find an example from these biblical passages that expresses the manner in which you want to bless others. _____

_____

_____

S State

What blessing from God or from others have you received this week?

_____

_____

S Share

Tell about some way in which you recently blessed someone.

_____

_____

II. New Testament References to Blessings and Benedictions

In the Greek New Testament text there are two primary words that are most often translated by the English words **bless, blessing, or blessed**. These words are *eulogeo* (literal meaning: "to speak well") and *makarios* (often translated "happy"). These terms occur some 60 times in the Gospels, most frequently in the Gospel of Luke. Many of these are repetitious since the Gospels record some of the same events and teachings.

In addition to these are some 37 benedictions in the New Testament which we will consider.

MATTHEW

We begin our study with 19 references in the Gospel of Mathew.

The first nine of these "blesseds" are popularly known as the Beatitudes, (sometimes called the Beautiful Attitudes); words spoken by Jesus as part of His Sermon on the Mount (Mathew 5-7). Actually, each of these is a **benediction**—a spoken blessing.

"**Blessed** are the poor in spirit, for theirs is the kingdom of heaven" (5:3).

To be "poor in spirit" means to be humble, recognizing our unworthiness of Yahweh's favor, and claiming His provisions for all our spiritual needs.

"**Blessed** are those who mourn, for they shall be comforted" (5:4).

We must "mourn" over our sins, confessing and forsaking them.

"**Blessed** are the meek, for they shall inherit the earth" (5:5).

Meekness is not weakness; rather it is power under control.

"**Blessed** are those who hunger and thirst for righteousness, for they shall be filled" (5:6).

All who have an appetite for being right with God will be satisfied with His provision.

"**Blessed** are the merciful, for they shall obtain mercy" (5:7).

The mercy we receive from Yahweh must be passed on to others.

"**Blessed** are the pure in heart, for they shall see God" (5:8).

Spiritual purity comes from His forgiveness and enables us to see God more clearly in life's experiences.

"**Blessed** are the peacemakers, for they shall be called the sons of God" (5:9).

We who have peace with God are to become "peacemakers" in all our relationships

"**Blessed** are those who are persecuted for righteousness sake, for theirs is the kingdom of heaven" (5:10).

Being different from the world will lead to mistreatment by the world.

"**Blessed** are you when they revile and persecute you, and say all kinds of evil against you falsely for My sake. Rejoice and be exceedingly glad, for great is your reward in heaven, for so they persecuted the prophets who were before you" (5:11-12).

Rather than feel resentment and self-pity when persecuted, we can be joyful, knowing our reward is great in heaven.

These nine blesseds (makarios) give an accurate description of the character and actions of Jesus Himself. Our only hope of expressing these same qualities is to allow Him to so control us that we become like Him.

5:44 "But I say to you, love your enemies, **bless** those who curse you, do good to those who hate you, and pray for those who spitefully use you and persecute you, that you may be sons of your Father in heaven."

Our response to mistreatment is to be loving, kind, and helpful to those who so treat us.

11:6 "And **blessed** is he who is not offended because of Me."

These words are among Jesus' response to those disciples of John the Baptist who came inquiring of Him.

13:16 "But **blessed** are your eyes for they see, and your ears for they hear; for assuredly, I say to you that many prophets and righteous men desired to see what you see, and did not see it, and to hear what you hear, and did not hear it."

Jesus spoke here regarding the benefit had by those who heard Him teach and witnessed His works. (Compare this to John 20:29.)

14:19 "The He commanded the multitudes to sit down on the grass. And He took the five loaves and the two fish, and looking up to heaven, He **blessed** and broke and gave the loaves to the disciples; and the disciples gave to the multitudes."

This was the occasion of Jesus feeding the 5,000.

16:17 "Jesus answered and said to him, '**Blessed** are you, Simon Bar-Jonah, for flesh and blood has not revealed this to you, but My Father who is in heaven.'"

Simon was blessed to have received the revelation of who Jesus was.

21:9 "Then the multitude who went before and those who followed cried out, saying: 'Hosanna to the Son of David! **Blessed** is He who comes in the name of the LORD! Hosanna in the highest!'"

The Triumphal Entry of Jesus into Jerusalem caused the multitudes to cry out these words from Psalm 118:26.

23:39 "For I say to you, you shall see Me no more till you say, '**Blessed** is He who comes in the name of the LORD!'"

As Jesus lamented over the people of Jerusalem who so often rejected Yahweh's efforts to instruct them, He quoted these words from Psalm 118:26.

24:46 "**Blessed** is that servant whom his master, when he comes, will find so doing."

Jesus' parable of the faithful servant and the evil one is the occasion for these words of commendation for being a good steward.

25:34 "Then the King will say to those on His right hand, 'Come you **blessed** of My Father, inherit the kingdom prepared for you from the foundation of the world.'"

These words of Jesus describe the rewards given to His righteous servants when He returns and judges the nations.

26:26 "And as they were eating, Jesus took bread, **blessed** it and broke it, and gave it to the disciples and said, 'Take, eat; this is My body.'"

These words were spoken by Jesus at His last supper with His disciples. Some translations use the words "gave thanks" instead of "blessed."

MARK

The writer of this gospel was also known as John Mark who was a cousin of Barnabas. The early church in Jerusalem met in the home of his mother, Mary. He probably gained much of his information about Jesus from Simon Peter.

We find seven occurrences of the terms bless and blessed in his writing.

6:41 "And when He had taken the five loaves and the two fish, He looked up to heaven, **blessed** and broke the loaves and gave them to His disciples to set before them; and the two fish He divided among them all."

This occasion is the miracle of the feeding of the 5,000, also recorded in Matthew 14:19.

8:7 "And they had a few small fish; and having **blessed** them, He said to set them also before them."

On this occasion there were 4,000 in the crowd. These are vivid examples of Jesus' compassion as well as His power over nature.

10:16 "And He took them up in His arms, put His hands on them and **blessed** them."

These were young children whom Jesus blessed in spite of His disciples' attempt to send them away.

11:9-10 "Then those who went before and those who followed cried out saying, 'Hosanna! **Blessed** is He who comes in the name of the LORD! **Blessed** is the kingdom of our father David that comes in the name of the Lord! Hosanna in the highest!'"

Here is a reference to Jesus' Triumphal Entry into the city of Jerusalem.

14:22 "And as they were eating, Jesus took bread, **blessed** it and broke it, and gave it to them and said, 'Take, eat; this is My body.'"

These were Jesus' words at the Last Supper.

14:61 "Again, the high priest asked Him, saying to Him, 'Are you the Christ, the Son of the **Blessed**?' And Jesus said, 'I am. And you will see the Son of Man sitting at the right hand of the Power, and coming with the clouds of heaven.'"

It was because of this claim that Jesus was condemned to die.

LUKE

Doctor Luke was a Gentile physician who joined Paul on his second missionary journey. Since he gives the most details about Mary, the mother of Jesus, and the few childhood references about Him, he probably interviewed Mary in order to compile information about the life of Jesus. He is also the writer of the Acts of the Apostles.

His gospel has the most (29) references to bless and blessing and blessed.

1:28 "And having come in, the angel said to her, 'Rejoice, highly favored one, the Lord is with you, **blessed** are you among women.'"

Here are the first words of the angel Gabriel to Mary; announcing her upcoming role as Jesus' mother,

1:46-48 "And Mary said, 'My soul magnifies the Lord, and my spirit has rejoiced in God my Savior. For He has regarded the lowly state of His maidservant; for behold, henceforth all generations will call me **blessed**.'"

This song of Mary expresses her sense of wonder at being chosen to give birth to the Messiah.

1:42, 45 "Then she (Elizabeth) spoke out with a loud voice and said, '**Blessed** are you among women, and **blessed** is the fruit of your womb! . . . . **Blessed** is she who believed, for there will be a fulfillment of those things which were told her from the Lord.'"

Mary's visit to her cousin Elizabeth was the occasion of these words of **benediction.**

1:68-69 "Now his father Zacharias was filled with the Holy Spirit and prophesied, saying: '**Blessed** is the Lord God of Israel, for He has visited and redeemed His people, and has raised up a horn of salvation for us in the house of His servant David.'"

These are the words of the father of John the Baptist given before the birth of his son.

2:28-34 "He took Him up in his arms and **blessed** God and said, 'Lord, now You are letting Your servant depart in peace, according to Your word; for my eyes have seen Your salvation which You have prepared before the face of all peoples.' . . . Then Simeon **blessed** them, and said to Mary His mother, 'Behold, this Child is destined for the fall and rising of many in Israel, and for a sign which will be spoken against.'"

Simeon was an old man who came often to the temple in Jerusalem. It had been revealed to him that before he died, he would see the Christ. These words of **benediction** and prophecy were spoken by him when he lifted up Jesus and spoke concerning Him.

6:20-23 "Then He lifted up His eyes toward the disciples, and said: '**Blessed** are you poor, for yours is the kingdom of God. **Blessed** are you who hunger now, for you shall be filled. **Blessed** are you who weep now, for you shall laugh. **Blessed** are you when men hate you, and when they exclude you, and revile you, and cast out your name as evil, for the Son of Man's sake. Rejoice in that day and leap for joy! For indeed your reward is great in heaven, for in like manner their fathers did to the prophets.'"

Here are four of the eight Beatitudes found in Mathew's gospel. Each one is actually a spoken **benediction.**

6:27-28 "But I say to you who hear: 'Love your enemies, do good to those who hate you. **Bless** those who curse you and pray for those who spitefully use you.'"

Another command to respond to one's enemies with kindness.

7:23 "'And **blessed** is he who is not offended in Me.'"

A repeat of Matthew 11:6.

9:16 "Then He took the five loaves and two fish, and looking up to heaven, He **blessed** and broke them, and gave them to the disciples to set before the multitude."

Here is Luke's account of the feeding of the 5,000.

10:23 "And He turned to His disciples and said privately, '**Blessed** are the eyes which see the things you see.'"

Mathew 13:16 records this same passage.

11:27-28 "And it happened as He spoke these things, that a certain woman from the crowd raised her voice and said to Him, '**Blessed** is the womb that bore You, and the breasts which nursed You!' But He said, 'More than that, **blessed** are those who hear the word of God and keep it.'"

Jesus turned attention from Himself and His mother in order to commend those who heard His word and chose to obey it.

12:37-38, 43 "**Blessed** are those servants whom the master, when he comes, will find watching. Assuredly, I say to you that he will gird himself and have them sit down to eat, and will come and serve them. And if he should come in the second watch, or come in the third watch, and find them so, **blessed** are those servants . . . . **Blessed is** that servant whom his master will find so doing when he comes.

Jesus commended faithful servants and promised rewards to them.

13:35 "'See! Your house is left to you desolate; and assuredly, I say to you, you shall not see Me until the time comes when you say, "**Blessed** is He who comes in the name of the LORD!"'"

The words were spoken to residents in the city of Jerusalem.

14:13-15 "'But when you give a feast, invite the poor, the maimed, the lame, the blind. And you will be **blessed**, because they cannot repay you, for you shall be repaid at the resurrection of the just.'"

These words of Jesus are among those He spoke to encourage His followers to reach out to those who could not help themselves.

19:38 "**Blessed** is the King who comes in the name of the LORD! Peace in heaven and glory in the highest!"

These words are a quote from Psalm 118:26, and were proclaimed by a crowd of people as Jesus approached Jerusalem in His Triumphal Entry.

23:29 "Jesus, turning to them said, 'Daughters of Jerusalem, do not weep for Me, but weep for yourselves and for your children. For indeed the days are coming when they will say, "**Blessed** are the barren, the wombs that never bore, and the breasts which never nursed."'"

These words are only in Luke's Gospel and were spoken by Jesus just prior to being nailed to a cross.

24:30 "Now it came to pass, as He sat at the table with them, that He took bread, **blessed** and broke it, and gave it to them. Then their eyes were opened and they knew Him; and He vanished from their sight."

Following His resurrection, Jesus joined two disciples as they walked from Jerusalem to their home in Emmaus. They invited Him to join them for the evening meal. As He took bread and blessed it, their eyes were opened to recognize Him.

24:50-51, 53 "And He led them out as far as Bethany, and He lifted up His hands and **blessed** them. Now it came to pass while He **blessed** them, that He was parted from them and carried up into heaven. And they worshiped Him, and returned to Jerusalem with great joy, and were continually in the temple praising and **blessing** God."

These final references occurred following Jesus' resurrection.

JOHN

The first three gospels are known as the Synoptic Gospels, meaning to see from the same perspective; they cover most of the same material. However, John, who may have read these earlier accounts, wanted to add more information. Thus his writing does not include such information as: the virgin birth, the baptism of Jesus, His temptations, the transformation, the Lord's Supper, His agony in the garden, or the ascension.

It is interesting to note that this gospel account only has two usages of our focus word "blessed." One of these is a repeat of what we have seen in Mathew and the others.

12:13 "Hosanna! **Blessed** is He who comes in the name of the LORD! The King of Israel!"

This is from John's account of the Triumphal Entry.

14:27 "Peace I leave with you, My peace I give to you; not as the world gives do I give to you. Let not your heart be troubled, neither let it be afraid."

Here is a beautiful **benediction** (a spoken blessing) from Jesus.

20:29 "Jesus said to him, 'Thomas, because you have seen Me, you have believed. **Blessed** are those who have not seen and yet have believed.'"

Only John records this conversation with Thomas. We, who have not seen Jesus but have believed, are included in this promise to be blessed.

STUDY GUIDE

Prepare your responses to these questions and share them with other learners.

B Biblical Reference

Choose your favorite Scripture reference from this session and list it here. _____

Be prepared to explain your reason for this choice. _____

_____

L Learning

What new or helpful truth have you learned from this session?

_____

_____

E Example

Find an example from these biblical passages that expresses the manner in which you want to bless others. _____

_____

_____

S State

What blessing from God or from others have you received this week?

_____

_____

S Share

Tell about some way in which you recently blessed someone.

_____

_____

ACTS

Doctor Luke is the probable writer of Acts, which thus becomes volume 2 of his Gospel. He apparently joined Paul and Silas on the second missionary journey. We will look at three references to bless and blessing here.

3:25-26 "You are sons of the prophets, and of the covenant which God made with the fathers, saying to Abraham, 'And in your seed all the families of the earth shall be **blessed**. To you first, God having raised up His Servant Jesus, sent Him to **bless** you in turning away every one of you from your iniquities.'"

These are Peter's words to the crowd that gathered following the healing of the lame man at the temple gate.

20:35 "I have shown you in every way, by laboring like this, that you must support the weak. And remember the words of the Lord Jesus, that He said, 'It is more **blessed** to give than to receive.'"

Paul spoke these words to the elders of the church from Ephesus. The words he quoted from Jesus are found only here.

ROMANS

Thirteen of the twenty-one epistles of the New Testament were written by the apostle Paul. This letter to the church members in Rome is one of these. It is the first New Testament book that identifies the writer. He dictated this manuscript to his disciple, Tertius (16:22), while they were in Corinth on the third missionary journey, around A.D. 57. Romans is Paul's doctrinal treatise, setting forth the fundamental truths of the gospel message. It also has a long practical section where he makes clear application of Christian doctrines to life situations. He also includes numerous **benedictions**, such as the one which we will examine first.

1:7 "To all who are in Rome, beloved of God, called to be saints: grace to you and peace from God our Father and the Lord Jesus Christ."

Paul begins his letter to the Romans with this simple, brief statement of blessing; he repeats these words several times in the thirteen letters which follow.

1:24-25 "Therefore God also gave them up to uncleanness, in the lusts of their hearts, to dishonor their bodies among themselves, who exchanged the truth of God for the lie, and worshiped and served the creature rather than the Creator, who is **blessed** forever. Amen"

The context of these words of rebuke describe the sinful acts of homosexuality which were practiced by the pagans in Rome, and elsewhere.

4:6-9 "David also describes the **blessedness** of the man to whom God imputes righteousness apart from works: '**blessed** are those who lawless deeds are forgiven, and whose sins are covered; **blessed** is the man to whom the LORD shall not impute sin.' Does this **blessedness** then come upon the circumcised only, or upon the uncircumcised also? For we say that faith was accounted to Abraham for righteousness."

Paul quotes from David in Psalm 32:1-2 to prove his point that righteousness comes through one's faith, apart from works.

9:5 ". . . . of whom are the fathers and from whom, according to the flesh, Christ came, who is over all, the eternally **blessed** God. Amen."

The apostle speaks here of the great sorrow he feels due to his fellow Israelite's decision to reject Christ who is their own kinsman.

12:14 "**Bless** those who persecute you; **bless** and do not curse."

This command is found among other similar ones regarding a Christian's response to mistreatment by others.

15:5-6 "Now may the God of patience and comfort grant you to be like-minded toward one another; according to Christ Jesus, that you may with one mind and one mouth glorify the God and Father of our Lord Jesus Christ."

Here is another beautiful **benediction** calling upon believers to exercise those virtues of Christ toward one another, all for the glory of God.

16:25-27 "Now to Him who is able to establish you according to my gospel and the preaching of Jesus Christ, according to the revelation of the mystery which was kept secret since the world began but now has been made manifest, and by the prophetic Scriptures has been made known to all nations, according to the commandment of the everlasting God for obedience to the faith—to God alone wise, be glory through Jesus Christ forever. Amen."

Typically, Paul ends his letters with a **benediction**. This is one of his longest and most interesting. Notice key words, such as "my gospel," "revelation of the mystery," "kept secret," and "made known to all nations." What a fitting conclusion to this doctrinal epistle!

FIRST CORINTHIANS

Paul wrote several letters to this church; some have been lost (5:9), but these two remain. His first visit there was on his second missionary journey around A.D. 52-53; this letter was sent from Ephesus (spring of A.D. 57) during his third missionary journey. He wrote to help correct various moral and fellowship problems. We look at two **benedictions** and four references to our key words.

1:3 "Grace to you and peace from God our Father and the Lord Jesus Christ."

Here is a brief **benediction**, similar to the one found in Romans 1:7, which is typical of Paul's introduction to his letters.

4:12 "And we labor, working with our own hands. Being reviled, we **bless**; being persecuted, we endure it."

Paul uses his own experience as a Christ-follower to challenge his readers to follow his example of how to deal with mistreatment.

10:16 "The cup of **blessing** which we **bless**, is it not the communion of the blood of Christ? The bread which we break, is it not the communion of the body of Christ?

Some of the Corinthians were participating in idol worship. Paul uses the Lord's Supper to remind them of the seriousness of using the cup and bread as a means of communicating with Christ; thus idolatry is forbidden.

14:16 "Otherwise, if you **bless** with the spirit, how will he who occupies the place of the uninformed say 'Amen' at your giving of thanks, since he does not understand what you say."

Here is Paul's warning to those who spoke in a language others could not understand. His appeal is to always speak in a clearly understandable manner.

16:23 "The grace of our Lord Jesus Christ be with you."

This closing **benediction,** like the opening one (1:3), emphasizes grace as the ultimate blessing of Jesus upon His followers.

SECOND CORINTHIANS

This epistle was written by Paul from Macedonia on his third journey (summer of A.D. 57). It was carried to them by Titus (8:6, 17). Paul's plan was to visit the Corinthians soon. This letter prepared them for his personal visit.

1:2-4 "Grace to you and peace from God our Father and the Lord Jesus Christ. **Blessed** be the God and Father of our Lord Jesus Christ, the Father of mercies and God of all comfort, who comforts us in all our tribulation that we may be able to comfort those who are in any trouble, with the comfort with which we ourselves are comforted by God."

Paul opens his letter with this beautiful **benediction**, focusing on God as the Comforter, whose comfort equips us to comfort one another.

9:8 "God is able to make all grace abound toward you, that you always having all sufficiency in all things, have an abundance for every good work."

The context for this **benediction** is the encouragement from Paul for Christians to be generous in giving. He promises that God will faithfully supply all we need to be liberal in our gifts to help others.

11:31 "The God and Father of our Lord Jesus Christ, who is **blessed** forever, knows that I am not lying."

As Paul enumerated all the various kinds of suffering he had endured, he felt the need to affirm the truthfulness of all he claimed.

13:14 'The grace of the Lord Jesus Christ, and the love of God, and the communion of the Holy Spirit be with you all. Amen"

This **benediction** forms the closing words of Paul's letter to the Corinthians. Notice the inclusion of the blessing of the Trinity (Father, Son, and Holy Spirit).

GALATIANS

Galatia was an area in central Asia Minor (modern Turkey), visited by Paul and Barnabas on their first missionary journey (A.D. 45-48). Later Paul returned to this area on his second and third journey. This letter was written by Paul, from Corinth or Ephesus or Macedonia around A.D. 57 as a circular document to be shared by churches in this area.

Paul wrote this epistle to warn against Judaizers and to affirm the true nature of the gospel.

1:3-5 "Grace to you and peace from God the Father and our Lord Jesus Christ, who gave Himself for our sins that He might deliver us from this present evil age according to the will of our God and Father, to whom be glory forever and ever. Amen."

Another opening **benediction,** very similar to Paul's introduction in other letters.

3:8-9 "And the Scripture, foreseeing that God would justify the nations by faith, preached the gospel to Abraham beforehand, saying, 'In you all the nations shall be **blessed**.' So then those who are of faith are **blessed** with believing Abraham."

Here is Paul's affirmation regarding the fact of sinners being made right (justified) with God by faith, not by keeping the Law.

4:15 "What then was the **blessing** you enjoyed? For I bear you witness that, if possible, you would have plucked out your own eyes and given them to me."

Again, the context helps us understand what Paul means here. He speaks of the strong affection the Galatians had for him, even to the extent of giving him their eyes in his affliction. (Some interpret this to refer to Paul's supposed eye disease that became a hindrance for him.)

6:18 "Brethren, the grace of our Lord Jesus Christ be with your spirit. Amen."

Paul followed his custom of closing this epistle with a **benediction.**

EPHESIANS

This is one of four epistles (Philippians, Colossians, and Philemon) written from Rome A.D. 61-63, while Paul was in prison there. He had planted this church on his third missionary journey, later returning there for an extended period of time. One strong theme of this letter is the unity Christ brings to Jews and Gentiles.

We examine the single occurrence of the term blessing, plus two **benedictions.**

1:3 "**Blessed** be the God and Father of our Lord Jesus Christ, who has **blessed** us with every spiritual **blessing** in the heavenly places in Christ."

The apostle opens his letter with these words of praise, celebrating the rich blessings He has bestowed upon His church.

3:20-21 "Now to Him who is able to do exceedingly abundantly above all that we ask or think, according to the power that works in us, to Him be glory in the church by Christ Jesus throughout all ages, world without end. Amen.

This **benediction** acknowledges the total sufficiency God supplies for us to do His will as He works mightily in and through us.

6:23-24 "Peace to the brethren, and love with faith, from God the Father and the Lord Jesus Christ. Grace be with all those who love our Lord Jesus Christ in sincerity. Amen.

Here is a typical manner in which Paul closes most of his letters—a **benediction** calling for peace, love, and faith.

PHILIPPIANS

Philippi was the first city in Europe to hear the gospel from Paul. He stopped there on his second missionary journey (A.D. 49). He wrote these words to thank them for sending him a financial gift to help during his imprisonment, probably in Rome. A recurring theme of this brief letter is that of a believer's joy, in spite of trials.

There are no occurrences of the words bless or blessing. However, consider the great blessing referred to in these words of **benediction:**

1:2 Grace to you and peace from God our Father and the Lord Jesus Christ.

Another typical **benediction** brings closure to this very personal letter.

4:19-20 "And my God shall supply all your need according to His riches in glory by Christ Jesus. Now to our God and Father be glory forever and ever. Amen.

A friend of mine once told me that the message of the entire Bible is summed up in these words from Philippians 4:19: *My God shall supply all your need according to His riches in glory in Christ Jesus.*

COLOSSIANS

Here is another of Paul's prison epistles, written around A.D. 61. He had never been to Colosse, but learned of their church from his co-worker Epaphras who brought news about them to Paul (1:7). Paul composed this letter to warn the Colossians about false teachers, and to declare the supremacy of Christ over all creation.

1:2 "To the saints and faithful brethren in Christ who are in Colosse: Grace to you and peace from God our Father and the Lord Jesus Christ."

Paul opens his brief letter with his usual pronouncement of a **benediction** upon them.

He closed his epistle with this simple **benediction**: "Grace be with you. Amen." (4:18)

STUDY GUIDE

Prepare your responses to these questions and share them with other learners.

B Biblical Reference

Choose your favorite Scripture reference from this session and list it here. _____

Be prepared to explain your reason for this choice. _____

_____

L Learning

What new or helpful truth have you learned from this session?

_____

_____

E Example

Find an example from these biblical passages that expresses the manner in which you want to bless others. _____

_____

_____

S State

What blessing from God or from others have you received this week?

_____

_____

S Share

Tell about some way in which you recently blessed someone.

_____

_____

FIRST THESSALONIANS

Paul spent three Sabbaths here on his second missionary journey (Acts 17:2). He wrote this letter to them from Corinth around A.D. 61-62. This is the only Bible book that specifically states that Christians who are alive on earth when Christ returns will be changed to resurrection life and be caught up to meet Him in the air without dying.

1:1b "Grace to you and peace from God our Father and the Lord Jesus Christ."

5:28 "The grace of our Lord Jesus Christ be with you. Amen."

Here are typical **benedictions** to introduce and conclude his letter.

3:12-13 "May the Lord make you increase and abound in love to one another and to all, just as we do to you, so that He may establish your hearts blameless in holiness before our God and Father at the coming of our Lord Jesus Christ with all His saints."

This **benediction** is in the form of a prayer that Paul offered for the Thessalonians.

5:23 "Now may the God of peace Himself sanctify you completely; and may your whole spirit, soul, and body be preserved blameless at the coming of our Lord Jesus Christ."

Here is another **benediction**-prayer offered by Paul for his readers.

SECOND THESSALONIANS

Paul wrote this second letter to correct a misunderstanding about the return of Jesus ("day of the Lord"). Some had quit their jobs because they expected Him to come back very soon. No reference to bless or blessings are here, but notice his usual opening words plus two notable **benedictions.**

1:2 "Grace to you and peace from God our Father and the Lord Jesus Christ."

2:16-17 "Now may our Lord Jesus Christ Himself, and our God and Father, who has loved us and given us everlasting consolation and good hope by grace, comfort your hearts and establish you in every good word and work."

The English words "consolation" and "comfort" in this **benediction** are the same word in Greek, and refer to the ministry of the Comforter-the Holy Spirit. Thus the full Trinity is included in this passage.

3:16-18 "Now may the Lord of peace Himself give you peace always in every way. The Lord be with you all. The salutation of Paul with my own hand, which is a sign in every epistle; so I write. The grace of our Lord Jesus Christ be with you all. Amen."

Notice this **benedictory** prayer for "the Lord of peace Himself" to "be with you all." We have peace, not as a separate gift, but by the presence with us of "the Lord of peace"; He **is** our peace. Thus, we never are without peace because we are never without Him.

FIRST TIMOTHY

This is the first of six New Testament epistles addressed to individuals rather to churches (! and 2 Timothy, Titus, Philemon, 2 and 3 John). In addition this is the first of three "Pastoral Epistles." First and Second Timothy and Titus were written by the apostle Paul to specific church leaders.

Paul wrote to young Timothy, who had become the pastor/leader of the Christians in Ephesus, in order to encourage him and give instructions regarding the organization of that church.

Two references to blessed are found here, along with three **benedictions.**

1:2 "To Timothy, my true son in the faith. Grace, mercy, and peace from God our Father and Jesus Christ our Lord."

Paul's traditional and initial **benediction** begins his letter to Timothy.

1:11 ". . . according to the glorious gospel of the **blessed** God which was committed to my trust."

God is here referred to as "the **blessed** God" because He is the ultimate source of all blessings.

1:17 " Now to the King eternal, immortal, invisible, to God who alone is wise, be honor and glory forever and ever. Amen."

This unique **benediction** gives a very comprehensive description of Yahweh. Notice the terms *eternal, immortal, invisible,* and *wise.* No wonder He deserves honor and glory forever.

6:14-16, 21 ". . . keep the commandment without spot, blameless until our Lord Jesus Christ's appearing which He will manifest in His own time. He who is the **blessed** and only Potentate, the King of kings and the Lord of lords, who alone has immortality, dwelling in unapproachable light, whom no man has seen or can see, to whom be honor and everlasting power. . . Grace be with you. Amen."

This closing **benediction** includes another reference to Yahweh as the "**blessed** and only Potentate."

SECOND TIMOTHY

Here is Paul's final letter written from his second imprisonment in Rome (1:8). He mentions the names of 23 persons, only Luke had access to him. He asked Timothy to come to him and bring his personal belongings (4:13).

1:2 "To Timothy, my beloved son; Grace, mercy, and peace from God the Father and Christ Jesus our Lord."

4:22 "The Lord Jesus Christ be with your spirit. Grace be with you. Amen."

As usual, Paul begins and closes this final letter with short **benedictions.**

TITUS

This letter of three brief chapters was written to Paul's associate, Titus, who was a Gentile. He had left Titus on the island of Cyprus to help the church there. Two brief and similar **benedictions** are found at the beginning and end of this epistle.

1:4 "Grace, mercy, and peace from God the Father and the Lord Jesus Christ, our Savior."

3:15 "The Lord Jesus Christ be with your spirit. Grace be with you. Amen."

PHILEMON

This very brief epistle is unique among biblical literature; it is a personal letter to a friend on behalf of another Christian brother. Onesimus had been the slave of Philemon. He stole from this master and ran away, ultimately meeting Paul in Rome where he was converted. Paul sent him back to Philemon with this letter in which Paul asked him to forgive and restore Onesimus as a Christian brother.

Again, find two short **benedictions.**

1:3 "Grace to you and peace from God our Father and the Lord Jesus Christ."

1:25 "The grace of our Lord Jesus Christ be with your spirit. Amen."

HEBREWS

The writer of this treatise is unknown, as well as the actual date of composition. The recipients were obviously Hebrew believers. It is a masterpiece of literature showing the superiority of the new covenant over the old. Consider numerous references to bless, blessed, and blessing.

6:7 "For the earth which drinks in the rain that often comes upon it, and bears herbs useful for those by whom it is cultivated receives **blessing** from God . . ."

The earth is blessed by the gift of rain from God, and the earth "drinks in the rain." What a testimony to the favor of God to His good earth.

6:13-14 "For when God made a promise to Abraham, because He could swear by no one greater, He swore by Himself, saying 'Surely, **blessing** I will **bless** you, and multiplying I will multiply you.'"

The writer quotes from Genesis 22:17 regarding God's promise to Abraham. There are more references to God's promises (18) in Hebrews than in any other book of the Bible. Every promise is a blessing.

7:1, 6-7 "For this Melchizedek, king of Salem, priest of the Most High God, who met Abraham returning from the slaughter of the kings and **blessed** him . . . but he whose genealogy is not derived from them received tithes from Abraham and **blessed** him who had the promise. Now beyond all contradiction the lessor is **blessed** by the better."

Only in Hebrews do we find Melchizedek in the New Testament. This reference regards his experience with Abraham found in Genesis 14. He is remembered for his act of blessing Abraham.

11:20-21 "By faith Isaac **blessed** Jacob and Esau concerning things to come. By faith Jacob, when he was dying, **blessed** each of the sons of Joseph, and worshiped, leaning on the top of his staff."

Here are references to two patriarchs who pronounced blessings upon their heirs. This was a common practice among these Old Testament family leaders.

12:17 "For you know that afterward, when he wanted to inherit the **blessing**, he was rejected, for he found no place for repentance, though he sought it diligently with tears."

The reference here is to Esau who sold his birthright to his brother Jacob for one meal. Here is a warning to those who fail to give proper value to a father's blessing.

13:20-21, 25 "Now may the God of peace who brought up our Lord Jesus from the dead, that great Shepherd of the sheep, through the blood of the everlasting covenant, make you complete in every good work to do His will, working in you what is well pleasing in His sight, through Jesus Christ, to whom be glory forever and ever. Amen . . . Grace be with you all. Amen"

The writer closes his masterpiece with a double **benediction**—one longer and one very brief—both very meaningful. The first **benediction** is a beautiful description of the work Yahweh has done in raising His Son, and in His work in His people. The second **benediction** reveals how these blessings come to us—His grace.

JAMES

The writer of this helpful book was James, the half-brother of Jesus, who became the leader of the church in Jerusalem. Probably written among the earliest New Testament documents (around A.D.45), it offers advice on practical Christian living with a strong emphasis on good works as evidence of authentic faith.

1:12 "**Blessed** is the man who endures temptation; for when he has been proved, he will receive the crown of life which the Lord has promised to those who love Him."

The blessedness of this man is that by enduring trials he will prove worthy of the reward of an abundant life.

1:25 "But he who looks into the perfect law of liberty and continues in it, and is not a forgetful hearer but a doer of the work, this one will be **blessed** in what he does."

James gives the promise of God's blessing upon the Christian who is "a doer of the work" not simply one who professes to believe.

3:8-10 "But no man can tame the tongue. It is an unruly evil, full of deadly poison. With it we **bless** our God and Father, and with it we curse men, who have been made in the similitude of God. Out of the same mouth proceed **blessing** and cursing. My brethren, these things ought not to be so."

These words come from a long passage regarding the power of one's speech. James calls for believers to gain control over all they say.

FIRST PETER

This letter has been known for its "theology of suffering," due to numerous references to the persecution Christians should expect to endure. Peter was one of the inner circle of Jesus' disciples (Peter, James, John). He follows the pattern of Paul's writings in that he opens and closes his epistle with **benedictions.**

1:2; 5:14 "Grace to you and peace be multiplied." "Peace to you all who are in Christ Jesus. Amen"

1:3 "**Blessed** be the God and Father of our Lord Jesus Christ, who according to His abundant mercy has begotten us again to a living hope through the resurrection of Jesus Christ from the dead, to an inheritance incorruptible and undefiled and that does not fade away reserved in heaven for you, who are kept by the power of God through faith for salvation ready to be revealed in the last time."

Here is a strong expression of the ultimate of all blessings that Yahweh has bestowed upon all believers.

3:8-9 "Finally, all of you be of one mind, having compassion for one another; love as brothers, be tenderhearted, be courteous; not returning evil for evil or reviling for reviling, but on the contrary **blessing**, knowing that you were called to this, that you may inherit a **blessing**."

Notice how Peter said that Christians are called to bless those who mistreat them, being compassionate, loving, courteous, and tenderhearted. In return they will receive, as an inheritance, God's blessing.

5:10-11 "But may the God of all grace, who called us to His eternal glory by Christ Jesus, after you have suffered a while, perfect, establish, strengthen, and settle you. To Him be the glory and the dominion forever and ever. Amen."

Here is Peter's closing **benediction** in the form of a doxology. Consider his prayer that the "God of all grace" would first allow us to suffer a while, but use such pain to make us stronger and better.

SECOND PETER

The apostle wrote this second letter several years after the first. His primary purpose was to warn believers of false teachers among them, and to assure the church of the certain return of Jesus. He begins with a powerful **benediction.**

1:2-3 "Grace and peace be multiplied to you in the knowledge of God and of Jesus our Lord, as His divine power has given to us all things that pertain to life and godliness, through the knowledge of Him who called us by glory and virtue . . ."

Peter opens his epistle with a strong statement regarding the fact that God has provided all that is needed for life and godliness.

STUDY GUIDE

Prepare your responses to these questions and share them with other learners.

B Biblical Reference

Choose your favorite Scripture reference from this session and list it here. _____

Be prepared to explain your reason for this choice. _____

_____

L Learning

What new or helpful truth have you learned from this session?

_____

_____

E Example

Find an example from these biblical passages that expresses the manner in which you want to bless others. _____

_____

_____

S State

What blessing from God or from others have you received this week?

_____

_____

S Share

Tell about some way in which you recently blessed someone.

_____

_____

FIRST JOHN

There are no benedictions or references to bless or blessing in First John, however, the author who probably was the apostle John, shares many blessed truths.

SECOND JOHN

John begins this brief letter with a **benedictory** greeting, much like the apostle Paul.

1:3 "Grace, mercy, and peace will be with you from God the Father and from the Lord Jesus Christ, the Son of the Father, in truth and love.

THIRD JOHN

This very brief note from the apostle John to Gaius, whom he calls "beloved" four times, has a **benediction**-like prayer in verse 2:

1:2 Beloved I pray that you may prosper in all things and be in health, just as your soul prospers.

JUDE

Like the writer of the book of James, Jude was another half-brother of Jesus, who did not become a disciple until the resurrection and ascension of Jesus. Later he became a leader in the church. He wrote these brief words to warn about false teachers in the church, and to encourage believers to stay true to the faith. He closed his letter with a memorable **benediction:**

1:24-25 "Now to Him who is able to keep you from stumbling. And to present you faultless before the presence of His glory with exceeding joy, to God our Savior, who alone is wise, be glory and majesty, dominion and power, both now and forever. Amen."

From these inspired words we come to understand that we are not able in and of ourselves to remain faithful to our Lord. Nor are we able to stand before Him as "faultless" persons, but the good news is: He is able! And He will keep us from falling away, that we may ultimately stand before His judgment seat fully acceptable to Him.

THE REVELATION

This final book of the New Testament was written by the apostle John during his imprisonment on the Isle of Patmos, some 35 miles off the coast of Asia Minor. The date was around A.D. 95, the last New Testament book written. The designated first readers were members of seven churches in Asia Minor. John wrote that which was revealed to him in a series of visions. It is called "the revelation of Jesus Christ which God gave Him to show His servants—things which must shortly take place" (1:1). Some 300 symbols are included to convey the meaning of this *unveiling*.

The most prominent figure of this amazing book is Jesus Christ, who is declared to be "the Lamb of God" some 26 times.

1:3 "**Blessed** is he who reads and those who hear the words of this prophecy, and keep those things which are written in it; for the time is near."

Here is the only time readers of a Bible book are declared to be blessed for reading, hearing, and doing what is therein recorded.

1:5-6 "Grace to you and peace from Him who is and who was and who is to come and from the seven spirits who are before His throne, and from Jesus Christ, the faithful witness, the firstborn from the dead and the ruler over the kings of the earth. To Him who loved us and washed us from our sins in His own blood and has made us kings and priests to His God and Father, to Him be glory and dominion forever and ever. Amen."

John's opening greeting includes this stately **benediction**, offering grace and peace from Jesus and "the seven spirits who are before His throne." Notice all the amazing undeserved benefits included in this declaration of blessing.

5:12-13 "Worthy is the Lamb who was slain to receive power and riches and wisdom, and strength and honor and glory and **blessing**! And every creature which is in heaven and on the earth and under the earth and such as are in the sea, and all that are in them, I heard saying: '**Blessing** and honor and glory and power, be to Him who sits on the throne and to the Lamb forever and ever!'"

These are the words that John heard from "many angels around the throne, the living creatures and the elders, and the number of them was ten thousand times ten thousand, and thousands of thousands." Along with every creature in heaven and on the earth, under the earth, and in the sea! What a huge throng of heavenly and earthly beings giving these words of praise and adoration.

7:11-12 "And all the angels stood around the throne and the elders and the four living creatures, and fell on their faces before the throne and worshiped God saying: 'Amen! **Blessing** and glory and wisdom, thanksgiving and honor and power and might, be to our God forever and ever. Amen.'"

This enormous multitude came from the Great Tribulation offering their tribute and praise in the form of a **benediction** to God.

14:13 "Then I heard a voice from heaven saying to me, 'Write: **Blessed** are the dead who die in the Lord from now on.' "Yes", says the Spirit, "that they may rest from their labors, and their works follow them."

For the first time, the dead believers are called blessed. Now they can rest and enjoy the rewards of their works.

16:15 "Behold, I am coming as a thief. **Blessed** is he who watches and keeps his garments, lest he walk naked and they see his shame."

These are the words of Jesus during the sixth bowl judgment.

19:9 "Then he said to me, 'Write: **Blessed** are those who are called to the marriage supper of the Lamb'; "And he said to me; 'These are the true sayings of God.'"

This voice came from God's throne, declaring the blessedness of those who are invited to the marriage supper of the Lamb.

20:6 "**Blessed** and holy is he who has part in the first resurrection. Over such the second death has no power, but they shall be priests of God and of Christ, and shall reign with Him a thousand years."

This is the only chapter in the Bible that mentions the millennium (thousand-year reign of Christ).

22:7 "Behold, I am coming quickly! **Blessed** is he who keeps the words of the prophecy of this book."

Here is a second promise of **blessing** to those who hear and keep the prophecies of this book (1:3).

22:14 "**Blessed** are those who do His commandments, that they may have the right to the tree of life, and may enter through the gates into the city."

An angel gave these words to John, who added them to this passage.

22:21 "The grace of our Lord Jesus Christ be with you all. Amen."

This is the final **benediction** of the Revelation and of the Bible.

Conclusion

Thus we complete a most interesting and significant survey of all the biblical references to the terms "bless," "blessing," and "blessed." (A total of some 585 occurrences.) What an amazing storehouse of these references to Yahweh's special favor upon His people and through His people upon others. Additionally, we have been repeatedly reminded of how blessed is our God. No other religion nor religious "sacred" writings has such a consistent focus on a god taking the initiative in reaching out and showing such favor. Here is one of the unique features of biblical revelation.

We also have examined some 65 benedictions found in both Old and New Testaments. These expressions of spoken blessings give additional emphasis to Yahweh's favor upon His people.

One significant fact surfaces through all these many references: All blessings have their origin with Yahweh, as a favorite doxology reminds us, "Praise God from whom all blessings flow. Praise Him all creatures here below. Praise Him above, ye heavenly hosts. Praise Father, Son, and Holy Ghost."

A Personal Benediction

Allow me to share with you an old hymn that declares a series of very helpful benedictions. I came across these beautiful words several years ago as I studied the stories of how various hymns came to be written. These words of prayer are very meaningful to me as I engage in a time of meditation and study to begin each day.

"May the Mind of Christ My Savior"

"May the mind of Christ my Savior live in me from day to day.
By His love and power controlling all I do and say.

--

May the Word of God dwell richly in my heart from hour to
hour, so that all may see I triumph only through His power.

--

May the peace of God my Father rule my life in everything,
that I may be able to comfort sick and sorrowing.

--

May the love of Jesus fill me, as the waters fill the sea; Him
exalting, self-abasing, this is victory.

--

May I run the race before me, strong and brave to face the foe,
looking only unto Jesus as I onward go.

--

May His beauty rest upon me, as I seek the lost to win, and may
they forget the channel, seeing only Him."

by Kate B. Wilkinson (1925)

To these good words, I have added the following:

"May I serve the Lord with gladness, reaching out to everyone.
Ever pointing them to Jesus as God's saving Son.

--

May the Holy Spirit fill me and His fruit be on display, making
a lasting difference in all I think and say.

--

May the name of Yahweh be revealed and its truth be fully
known, through the words we have spoken and the seeds we
have sown.

--

May the soon return of Jesus be upon my mind today, and may
this truth prepare me to please Him in every way.

STUDY GUIDE

Prepare your responses to these questions and share them with other learners.

B Biblical Reference

Choose your favorite Scripture reference from this session and list it here. _____

Be prepared to explain your reason for this choice. _____

_____

L Learning

What new or helpful truth have you learned from this session?

_____

_____

E Example

Find an example from these biblical passages that expresses the manner in which you want to bless others. _____

_____

_____

S State

What blessing from God or from others have you received this week?

_____

_____

S Share

Tell about some way in which you recently blessed someone.

_____

_____

Songs for the study of
"Bible Blessings and Benedictions"

"Make Me a Blessing"

1. Out in the highways and byways of life, many are weary and sad;

Carry the sunshine where darkness is rife, making the sorrowing glad.

Chorus: Make me a blessing, make me a blessing, out of my life may Jesus shine;

Make me a blessing O Savior I pray, Make me a blessing to someone today.

2. Tell the sweet story of Christ and His love, tell of His power to forgive;

Others will trust Him if only you prove true, every moment you live.

3. Give as 'twas given to you in your need, love as the Master loved you;

Be to the helpless a helper indeed, unto your mission be true.

"The Doxology"

Praise God from whom all blessings flow; Praise Him all creatures here below. Praise Him above ye heavenly host; Praise Father, Son, and Holy Ghost. Amen.

"Make Me a Channel of Blessing"

1. Is your life a channel of blessing? Is the love of God flowing through you? Are you telling the lost of the Savior? Are you ready His service to do?

Chorus: Make me a channel of blessing today. Make me a channel of blessing, I pray; my life possessing, my service blessing. Make me a channel of blessing today.

2. Is your life a channel of blessing? Are you burdened for those who are lost? Have you urged upon those who are straying, the Savior who died on the cross?

3. We cannot be channels of blessing if our lives are not free from known sin; we will barriers be and a hindrance to those we are trying to win.

"Bless His Holy Name"

[Chorus:]
Bless the Lord, O my soul,
and all that is within me,
bless His holy name.

[Verse:]
He has done great things,
He has done great things,
He has done great thing,
bless His holy name

"There Shall Be Showers of Blessing"

There shall be showers of blessing:
This is the promise of love;
There shall be seasons refreshing,
Sent from the Savior above.

Showers of blessing,
Showers of blessing we need;
Mercy-drops round us are falling,
But for the showers we plead.

There shall be showers of blessing-
Precious reviving again;
Over the hills and the valleys,
Sound of abundance of rain.

There shall be showers of blessing;
Send them upon us, O Lord!
Grant to us now a refreshing;
Come, and now honor Thy Word.

There shall be showers of blessing;
O that today they might fall,
Now as to God we're confessing,
Now as on Jesus we call!
There shall be showers of blessing,
If we but trust and obey;
There shall be seasons refreshing,
If we let God have His way.

"Blessed Be The Name"

All praise to Him who reigns above
In majesty supreme,
Who gave His Son for man to die,
That He might man redeem!

Refrain:
Blessed be the name! Blessed be the name!
Blessed be the name of the Lord!
Blessed be the name! Blessed be the name!
Blessed be the name of the Lord!

His name above all names shall stand,
Exalted more and more,
At God the Father's own right hand,
Where angel hosts adore.

Redeemer, Savior, friend of man
Once ruined by the fall,
Thou hast devised salvation's plan,
For Thou hast died for all.
His name shall be the Counselor,
The mighty Prince of Peace,
Of all earth's kingdoms conqueror,
Whose reign shall never cease.

"Count Your Blessings"

When upon life's billows you are tempest tossed,
When you are discouraged, thinking all is lost,
Count your many blessings, name them one by one,
And it will surprise you what the Lord hath done.

Refrain
Count your blessings, name them one by one,
Count your blessings, see what God hath done!
Count your blessings, name them one by one,
And it will surprise you what the Lord hath done.

Are you ever burdened with a load of care?
Does the cross seem heavy you are called to bear?
Count your many blessings, every doubt will fly,
And you will keep singing as the days go by.

When you look at others with their lands and gold,
Think that Christ has promised you His wealth untold;
Count your many blessings. Wealth can never buy
Your reward in heaven, nor your home on high.
So, amid the conflict whether great or small,
Do not be disheartened, God is over all;
Count your many blessings, angels will attend,
Help and comfort give you to your journey's end.

CPSIA information can be obtained
at www.ICGtesting.com
Printed in the USA
LVHW110034031218
598893LV00005B/130/P

9 781641 517003